W9-AQI-167

The Future of Turkish-Western Relations

Toward a Strategic Plan

Zalmay Khalilzad

Ian O. Lesser

F. Stephen Larrabee

RAND

Center for Middle East Public Policy • *National Security Research Division*

Prepared for the Smith Richardson Foundation

At the dawn of a new century, Turkish-Western relations have also entered a new era. Recent years have seen enormous changes within Turkish society. Turkish foreign policy horizons have expanded, and the country has developed a more active and sovereignty-conscious approach to nearby regions and relations with allies. Europe too has changed. With the Helsinki Summit decisions, the European Union (EU) has moved from a decidedly ambivalent stance to a more integrationist approach in its relations with Turkey. NATO—a key institutional link for Turkey in the West—is changing in ways that heighten Turkey's value to the Alliance. At the same time, the EU is developing foreign and defense policy initiatives in which Ankara's role remains uncertain. For the United States, Turkey's geopolitical importance is clear, but a predictable strategic relationship remains elusive, largely because Ankara and Washington have yet to develop a truly common agenda for relations in the post–Cold War world.

Against this background, this report explores the changing parameters of Turkish-Western relations and offers an agenda for closer strategic cooperation in the U.S.-Turkish-European triangle.

This study was undertaken with the generous support of the Smith Richardson Foundation, together with research funds provided by RAND's Center for Middle East Public Policy (CMEPP), and was carried out within the International Security and Defense Policy Center of RAND's National Security Research Division. CMEPP analyzes political, social, economic, and technological developments in the Middle East and assesses their implications for the region and beyond. RAND's National Security Research Division conducts research for the U.S. Department of Defense, for other U.S. government agencies, and other institutions.

CONTENTS

Preface iii

Figures vii

Summary ix

Acknowledgments xiii

Chapter One
    INTRODUCTION 1
    New Stakes, New Opportunities 1
    Structure of the Report 4

Chapter Two
    CHANGES ON THE TURKISH DOMESTIC SCENE AND
    THEIR FOREIGN POLICY IMPLICATIONS 5
    Rising Nationalism and Its Counterweights 5
    Traditional Versus Modern Worldviews 14
    Emergence of a Dynamic Private Sector 16
    A More Stable Internal Environment? 19

Chapter Three
    TURKISH FOREIGN AND SECURITY POLICY: NEW
    DIMENSIONS AND NEW CHALLENGES 21
    The Russian Factor 22
        Cyprus 23
        The Kurdish Issue 23
        Conventional Forces in Europe (CFE) 23
        Chechnya 24
    Central Asia and the Caucasus 25
    The Caucasus 28

The Middle East   31
The Balkans   36
Relations with Europe   39
NATO and ESDI   41
Greece and Cyprus   43
The American Connection   45
Conclusion: Turkey's Strategic Options   48

Chapter Four
WESTERN INTERESTS IN A CHANGING TURKEY   53
Transregional Issues and Opportunities   53
Changing Definition of European Security   54
New Security Geometries   56
A Pivotal State?   57
Thinking Through U.S. Stakes   61
   Stability and Democracy   61
   A Positive Regional Actor   65
   Enhancing U.S. Freedom of Action   71
Elements of Continuity and Change   75
Policy Implications   77

Chapter Five
A STRATEGIC PLAN FOR WESTERN-TURKISH
RELATIONS   79
The Impact of the End of the Cold War   79
Elements of a New Strategic Partnership Between the
   United States, Western Europe, and Turkey   82
   Energy Security   82
   Countering the Threat of Weapons of Mass Destruction
      and Missiles   86
   "Congage" Russia   89
   Deepening Turkish Integration in the West   93
Conclusion   95

FIGURES

1. Turkey-Persian Gulf and Caspian Basin   86

Turkish society, politics, and economy have evolved substantially over the past decades. The pace of this change has increased in recent years, and has included the rise of a much wider and more active debate on foreign and security policy—with new dimensions and new actors. These changes have important implications for Turkish policy, and the future of relations with the West. In this context, three developments have special meaning: (1) the rise of Turkish nationalism and greater sensitivity to sovereignty issues; (2) the polarization of traditional and modern elements in Turkish society; and (3) the emergence of a dynamic private sector, offering a new constellation of interlocutors in relations with the United States and Europe.

Turkey's external policy is also undergoing revision and redefinition in response to regional challenges and opportunities. Turkey will have a number of options in terms of foreign policy focus—European, Eurasian, Middle Eastern—as well as the possibility of concentration on the bilateral relationship with the United States The most likely outcome is a more multidimensional approach based strongly on Turkish national interests. Relations with the West will remain the core orientation, but with a more capable and assertive engagement elsewhere—generally, but not always, pursued in a multilateral frame.

Western stakes in Turkey continue to evolve in the post–Cold War era. As both European and U.S. strategy shifts to focus on the periphery of Europe, Turkey looms larger as a "pivotal state." The United States and Europe will have a strong stake in Turkish stability and democracy—crucial elements if Ankara is to play a more capable and positive regional role. In an era of power projection, the United States in particular will wish to see Turkey foster U.S. freedom of action in adjacent regions. To the extent that the European Union (EU) develops a more independent and concerted foreign and security policy, Turkey can also play this role in support of European interests—if the character of Turkish-European relations encourages this.

The future outlook will turn critically on a shared sense of strategic purpose between Turkey and the West. During the Cold War, Turkey played a critical role in the containment of Soviet power. There was agreement between the United States and West Germany, in particular, on the central importance of Turkey in Western strategy. A similar recognition of the Turkish role generated support and assistance for Turkey on Capitol Hill. As a result, although there were episodic problems in U.S.-Turkish relations, for much of the Cold War, Turkey was a major recipient of U.S. economic and military assistance.

With the end of the Cold War, the geopolitical environment and strategic priorities changed. For much of the past decade it has been unclear what Turks, Americans, and Europeans, as one, have been for and against. Security debates in the United States and Europe acknowledge Turkey's geopolitical significance and the need to reinvigorate relations with Turkey. But there has been relatively little progress in defining what a new agenda for strategic cooperation between Turkey and the West should include.

This report suggests that a new strategic agenda for Turkish-Western relations should focus on four key areas. These hardly exhaust the list of important areas for cooperation, but each in its way illustrates regions and issues where stakes are shared; where successful management will be important to the security and prosperity of Turkey, Europe, and the United States, and where Ankara has a natural and significant role to play.

The first item on the agenda concerns energy security. Turkey occupies a unique position adjacent to globally important oil and gas resources in the Persian Gulf, the Caucasus, and Central Asia, and astride alternative routes for bringing these resources to world markets. Access to adequate energy supplies at acceptable prices will also be essential to Turkey's own development over the longer term.

Second, Turkey and the West have a special stake in countering the proliferation of ballistic missiles of increasing range, as well as weapons of mass destruction. Since the Gulf War, Ankara and Washington have been at the forefront among the Western allies in focusing on this troubling trend. For the moment, Turkey is the NATO ally most clearly exposed to missile systems based in the Middle East, but this is rapidly emerging as a more widely shared vulnerability for Europe as a whole. Addressing these risks, through common policies, and by integrating Turkey in a future ballistic missile defense architecture, should be high on a new agenda, tailored to new challenges.

Third, Turkey is also most exposed to the security consequences of alternative Russian futures. Ankara would be on the front line in any renewed competition between Russia and the West, and today's potential areas for regional friction involving Moscow—from the Balkans and the eastern Mediterranean to the Caucasus, Central Asia, and the Gulf—are close to Turkey. Of more immediate concern, Turkey is exposed to the spillover effects of turmoil in Russia and the former Soviet Union, including refugee movements, transnational crime, and ethnic conflict around the Black Sea. Ankara seeks reassurance from the West in dealing with a potentially more difficult Russia. As a leading economic partner, Turkey can also be part of a more active and positive engagement with a reforming, cooperative Russia. In either case, a concerted strategy toward Russia must be part of a future triangular agenda.

Finally, the United States, as well as Europe, actively needs to ensure that the path toward closer Turkish integration in Europe remains open and anchors Turkey irreversibly to the West. The United States will have a strong stake in this process, and its interests will be undermined along with Ankara's if the EU's Helsinki decisions provide only a "hollow candidacy" for Turkey.

ACKNOWLEDGMENTS

This study benefited from discussions with numerous official and unofficial observers in Turkey, Europe, and the United States. We also wish to thank RAND colleagues who contributed to our analysis and helped facilitate our research: in particular Jerrold Green, Rachel Swanger, and Barbara Kliszewski. We are especially grateful to Marin Strmecki, Nadia Schadlow, and Samantha Ravich of the Smith Richardson Foundation for their interest and support, and to Philip Gordon at the Brookings Institution and Sabri Sayari at Georgetown University for their thoughtful comments on an earlier version of this report. Any errors or omissions are, of course, the responsibility of the authors.

Chapter One

INTRODUCTION

NEW STAKES, NEW OPPORTUNITIES

At the start of the 21st century, Western attention to Turkey is at a high point. Developments in Turkey, and in adjacent regions, compel attention. This reality contrasts with the fear of post–Cold War neglect widely expressed by Turkish observers after the fall of the Soviet Union and the collapse of the communist states in the East. The Gulf War refocused Western attention on Turkey, but like the previous context of the containment of Soviet power, it did so in a derivative way. Turkey was important as a result of its position on the map rather than its potential as a regional actor and partner in its own right. For many Turks, the Gulf War experience and the country's subsequent role in the containment of Iraq have reinforced the perception that Western policy (especially U.S. policy) toward Turkey is actually a product of other more important policies—Russia policy, Caspian policy, Balkan policy, Middle East policy, and so on. Recent changes within Turkey increasingly compel analysts and policymakers to see Turkey as a pivotal international actor in its own right.[1]

It is sometimes remarked that Turkey suffers from the lack of an effective lobby in Washington. The nature of U.S.-Turkish relations since 1945 suggests that this observation misses the mark. Turkey has indeed had a potent "lobby" in the form of the U.S. government:

---

[1]Some of these changes were anticipated in Graham E. Fuller, Ian O. Lesser, et al., *Turkey's New Geopolitics: from the Balkans to Western China*, Boulder, CO: Westview/RAND, 1993.

in particular, foreign and security policy decisionmakers who have consistently acknowledged the country's strategic importance, regardless of the state of bilateral relations. Turkey has consistently been portrayed as a country "too important to neglect." Given the frequent turmoil in Turkish politics, stability and instability in Turkey have been seen as having wider implications for the future of societies elsewhere. Thus, in the post–Cold War period, Turkey has been seen, variously, as (1) a model for states in the Caucasus, Central Asia, and the Balkans; (2) a harbinger of the rise or decline of Islamist movements in the Middle East; and (3) a key test of the effect of a dynamic private sector on political stability and reform. In all of these roles, Turkey is of keen interest for a U.S. foreign policy that has come to focus heavily on notions of "democratic enlargement" and human rights.

For Europe, the relationship with Turkey has always been complex. For centuries, Turkey has been a part—sometimes a critical part—of the European system; that is, part of the pattern of European political, economic, and security relations. The question of whether Turkey is part of Europe in the narrower sense of cultural and political identity, and even part of the European project of recent decades, is far less clear. Despite a strong preference for a European orientation since the founding of the Republic, Turkey's own sense of identity in this regard has varied with time. This sense of ambiguity and ambivalence in relations between Europe and Turkey remains, even in the wake of the European Union (EU) Helsinki Summit of December 1999. The summit declared Turkey a candidate for eventual EU membership, and is rightly seen as an important turning point in the very mixed history of recent relations between Ankara and Brussels. But Helsinki raises as many questions as it resolves. Is Europe serious about the prospect of Turkish membership? Can the EU deal effectively with economic, political, and "scale" challenges posed by Turkish integration? Is Turkey really prepared for the compromises on national sovereignty that closer relations with Brussels imply? Even short of full membership, what role will Turkey play in a Europe bent on developing a more concerted set of foreign and defense policies? In short, the issue of Turkey's relationship with Europe— always a leading economic partner, and increasingly much more than that—has acquired new significance with changes in Europe.

As Turkey has become more capable—and assertive—in diplomatic, economic, and military terms, Ankara has emerged as a more significant strategic partner for the West in troubled parts of the world, from the Balkans to Central Asia and the Middle East. The post–Cold War tendency toward a multilateral approach in U.S. foreign policy reinforces this point. Turkey is in the unusual position of being both a contributor to European security in a formal, Alliance context, and a partner in addressing wider problems influencing European, Middle Eastern, and Eurasian security, most of which lie outside the NATO area. As maintaining European security at its "core" becomes less challenging, and as Allies focus more heavily on security challenges on the periphery, Turkey will be a more important part of this equation. Moreover, many of the direct risks facing NATO today are actually on Turkey's borders.

Yet recognition of Turkey's strategic importance on both sides of the Atlantic is not synonymous with a new and stronger strategic relationship between Ankara and the West. Security debates in the United States and Europe acknowledge Turkey's geopolitical significance and the need to reinvigorate relations with Turkey. But there has been relatively little progress in defining what a new agenda for strategic cooperation between Turkey and the West should include. As Ankara has become more active on the regional scene, and more sovereignty conscious, it has become evident that a perception of shared interest and purpose is critical to a predictable, cooperative relationship. Turkey's location adjacent to areas of critical interest for the West is just the starting point for a strategic relationship. It is not sufficient in its own right. The West must understand Turkey's strategic perspective, and Turks must want to be engaged in U.S. and European policies toward the region. Absent a catalyzing and common threat (as in the Cold War), a concerted strategic approach can only be developed through a deeper strategic dialogue—and, more significantly, a new, relevant agenda.

Although this analysis places considerable emphasis on the relationship between Washington and Ankara, the triangular nature of the relationship is, arguably, more important than ever. The emerging relationship between Turkey and the West is likely to be more balanced vis-à-vis Europe and the United States than at any time in the past, and certainly more balanced than during the Cold War. To this extent, it is also more difficult to discuss the future of U.S. relations with Turkey outside the broader and even more important context of the transatlantic relationship as a whole.[2] In the most extreme case, a decoupling of transatlantic security would pose stark dilemmas for Ankara, especially if Turkey remains outside emerging European defense initiatives. In the more likely case, Turkey may wish to hedge between its ties to the United States as a predominant, multiregional superpower and its ties to the EU as a predominant economic partner with growing international aspirations. In any case, the future character of transatlantic relations will form a key context for Turkey's evolving relationship with the West.

STRUCTURE OF THE REPORT

Chapter Two examines the most important trends on the Turkish internal scene in recent years, their consequences for Turkish foreign policy, and their meaning for the United States and Europe. Chapter Three looks in detail at developments in regions surrounding Turkey and charts the prospects for Turkish foreign and security policy. Chapter Four critically examines Turkey's geopolitical importance from a Western perspective, analyzes the nature of the U.S. stakes in Turkey, and concludes with observations about what endures, what has changed, and what is likely to change in the 21st century. Finally, Chapter Five concludes by offering a strategic agenda for Turkish relations with the West, including policy recommendations. In addition to primary and secondary sources, throughout, the authors have relied on extensive discussions with official and unofficial observers in Turkey, Europe, and the United States.

---

[2]A full discussion of this broader question is beyond the scope of this report. For a recent analysis, see David C. Gompert and F. Stephen Larrabee (eds.), *America and Europe: A Partnership for A New Era*, New York: Cambridge University Press, 1997. To compare with a similar study from the early 1990s, see Nanette Gantz and John Roper (eds.), *Towards a New Partnership: U.S.-European Relations in the Post–Cold War Era*, Paris: Western European Union Institute for Security Studies/RAND, 1993.

Chapter Two

CHANGES ON THE TURKISH DOMESTIC SCENE AND THEIR FOREIGN POLICY IMPLICATIONS

Ian O. Lesser

Turkish society, politics, and economy have changed considerably over the past decades, with important implications for relations with the United States and the West as a whole. The pace of this change became especially rapid in the Özal years, driven along by economic reform, high growth rates, and new political currents. In this same period, key elements of the Atatürkist tradition that guided Turkish perceptions and policies since the foundation of the Republic—secularism, Western orientation, and statism—have come under severe strain. From the perspective of U.S.-Turkish relations, three aspects of domestic change are particularly significant: (1) the rise of Turkish nationalism; (2) the polarization of "traditional" and "modern" elements in Turkish society; and (3) the emergence of a dynamic private sector (and a new constellation of interlocutors for engagement with the United States).

RISING NATIONALISM AND ITS COUNTERWEIGHTS

A strong sense of Turkish nationalism was always imbedded within the Atatürkist vision, and was closely tied to the modernization and Westernization of the country.[1] The basic assumptions underpin-

---

[1]Some characteristics of this Turkish nationalism, including its basis in 19th-century European forms, are discussed in Ernest Gellner, *Encounters with Nationalism*, Oxford: Blackwell, 1994, pp. 81–91. See also Hugh Poulton, *Top Hat, Grey Wolf and Crescent*, New York: NYU Press, 1997.

ning Atatürkism and the Turkish sense of nationalism have been widely shared among Turkish elites in the period of the Republic.[2] The impressive electoral performance of the Nationalist Action Party (MHP) led by Devlet Bahceli in Turkey's 1999 general elections has focused interest on Turkish nationalism both inside and outside Turkey. In fact, a more vigorous nationalist sentiment has been visible on the Turkish scene for some time. The decade of the 1990s saw the emergence of independent Turkic republics of the former Soviet Union, and stimulated a lively debate in Turkey over the prospects for new ties based on ethnic affinity in the Caucasus and Central Asia, even embracing a larger region, from the Balkans to Western China. This pan-Turkist potential was taken up by fringe elements on the nationalist right (including MHP), and was embraced in a milder form, emphasizing trade and cultural ties, by mainstream parties as well as Turkey's active business community. In this same period, the emergence of an increasingly violent Kurdish insurgency in southeastern Anatolia, led by the Kurdistan Workers Party (PKK), and a more general rise in Kurdish political activism encouraged a nationalist reaction across the political spectrum. This reaction continues today, despite the waning of the PKK challenge, and was evident in the wake of the capture and trial of the PKK leader Abdullah Öcalan. The Öcalan affair, in particular, served as a rallying point for those who have been directly affected by the war against the PKK which may have claimed as many as 40,000 victims on all sides.

The nationalist impulse has been reinforced by the post–Gulf War experience and Turkey's frustration in its relations with the European Union (EU). There is an enduring perception among the public and elites alike that Turkey's forward-leaning, pro-Western stance in the conflict with Iraq has imposed significant economic and political costs on Turkey. Iraq had been Turkey's largest trading partner, and Ankara has been uncomfortable with containment policies that restrict its own economic and diplomatic freedom of action with Middle Eastern neighbors. Above all, Turks are wary of Western, espe-

---

[2]One scholar views the Turkish case as an example of nationalism that has become pervasive or "hegemonic" as an ideology of choice in key Middle Eastern states. See Ian S. Lustick, "Hegemony and the Riddle of Nationalism," in Leonard Binder (ed.), *Ethnic Conflict and International Politics in the Middle East,* Gainesville, FL: University Press of Florida, 1999.

cially U.S., intentions with regard to northern Iraq. Turkish analysts often refer to the "Sèvres syndrome," or the fear of containment and dismemberment, along the lines envisioned but never implemented by the Western powers after World War I. Even in moderate, well-informed circles, this residual concern encourages the view that Turkey needs to look after its own interests in a more vigorous way; that without considerable vigilance on the part of policymakers in Ankara, Turkish sovereignty and national interests may be "sold out," even by strategic partners in the West. Northern Iraq, closely tied to the Kurdish issue and Kurdish separatism, is the most sensitive example, but similar arguments can be heard in relation to Western appeasement of Russia, Syria, or Greece at Turkey's expense.

Flux in Turkey's relations with the EU has, at key junctures, fueled nationalist sentiment across a surprisingly wide spectrum of Turkish opinion. Turkey's ambition to "join" Europe in the sense of full membership in the EU suffered repeated setbacks in the 1990s, and has only recently been restored with the formal acceptance of Turkey's status as a candidate for membership at the EU's December 1999 Helsinki summit.[3] Ankara's involvement in the Gulf War coalition did not pay dividends in terms of European integration, despite Özal's best efforts. The reintegration of eastern and central Europe placed the issue of "who is European" in sharper relief, to the detriment of Turkey's European aspirations. Turkey, as a long-standing associate member of the EU, saw former communist states in the east move ahead of Turkey in the membership queue. The Luxembourg summit made clear that the EU did not even contemplate the start of an accession process for Turkey. As a consequence, even the most Western-oriented Turkish elites became bitter and disillusioned about Europe, and increasingly receptive to the idea of a more sovereignty-conscious and independent Turkey. This sense of resentment could be seen in the most diverse quarters, from the military and much of the business community, to the religious and secular right wing, and also on the left. Given the pressure that the EU had been applying on Ankara with regard to human rights, Cyprus, and other issues, it was even argued that the post-Luxembourg

---

[3]See Barry Buzan and Thomas Diez, "The European Union and Turkey," *Survival*, Vol. 4, No. 1 (Spring 1999), pp. 41–57; and Ian O. Lesser, *Bridge or Barrier? Turkey and the West After the Cold War*, Santa Monica, CA: RAND, R-4204-AF/A, 1992.

summit break in relations with Brussels provided Turkey with a useful breathing space, to pursue a more diversified foreign policy and to address domestic problems without external pressure.[4] In this as in many other areas, the August 1999 earthquake may well have helped to change attitudes toward EU-Turkish relations even prior to the Helsinki summit. Certainly, the experience produced calls on all sides for improved relations and the removal of practical impediments, such as the long-standing hold on EU economic assistance for Turkey.

The Helsinki summit has clearly effected a fresh chapter in Turkish-EU relations. It has also refocused the question of Turkish nationalism for the future. A Turkish elite and public that have grown accustomed to a more vigorous assertion of Turkish nationalism—often in opposition to European preferences—now find themselves with a renewed European perspective. This perspective is appealing to Western-oriented Atatürkists and to an increasingly materialistic middle class. It is also appealing to those traditionally on the margins of Turkish society and politics, including Islamists and Kurds, who see in Europe the possibility of more tolerance and freedom of action for their own views. Thus, the longer-term prospect opened by Helsinki serves as a counterweight to the recent growth of nationalist sentiment. However, it does not resolve Turkey's basic nationalist dilemma which, in some respects, has become more profound with Turkey's EU candidacy.

So far, Turkey's leadership and society have not had to confront the dilemma posed by a strong nationalist tradition and a powerful attachment to state sovereignty, on the one hand, with the prospect of integration in a sovereignty-diluting Europe, on the other. Even short of full EU membership—a very distant prospect for Turkey, at best—candidacy implies greater scrutiny, convergence, and compromise. From the most mundane (e.g., food regulations) to high politics (human rights, foreign and security policy), a closer relationship with formal EU structures will threaten Turkish sovereignty at many levels. This process has not been easy, even for core European states. How much more difficult will it be for a country where 19th-century notions of nationalism and sovereignty are still prevalent?

---

[4]Ilter Turan, "Towards Reconstruction," *Private View* (Istanbul), Autumn 1998, p. 11.

Looking ahead, even a multispeed, "variable geometry" Europe will impose significant sovereignty constraints on states that wish to take part. Through the customs union and other mechanisms, Turkey is already within this EU orbit. With the progress of Turkey's candidacy it will be increasingly difficult for Ankara to choose nationalist options if it wishes to remain on track for eventual EU membership.

In different ways, the Armenian-Azeri conflict over Nagorno-Karabakh, the Bosnia crisis, and recurring tensions with Greece (especially over Cyprus) have also strengthened the nationalist impulse, although these too are balanced by recent countervailing trends. Along with the Kurdish question, Cyprus is the nationalist issue par excellence, and tensions over the planned deployment of Russian surface-to-air missiles on the Greek side, and other flashpoints at the end of the 1990s, touched on nationalist sensitivities. The perception of Western inaction in Bosnia, where Turkish affinities were engaged, offered yet another basis for Turkish disillusionment with the West and reinforced the perception of Turkish "otherness" on the periphery of Europe.

Yet, as the Kosovo crisis illustrated, Ankara has opted for a multilateral approach to sensitive crises in the Balkans. "Earthquake diplomacy" played a role in defusing public opinion on frictions with Greece, and the post-Helsinki thaw in Greek-Turkish relations has only been possible because the nationalist critics of regional détente (on both sides) have been held in check by forward-looking leaderships. Even with regard to the crisis in Chechnya, where public sympathy for the Chechens could be expected to encourage a more assertive line, Ankara has reacted cautiously. One explanation for this caution is Ankara's interest in discouraging separatist movements and cross-border confrontations that could have uncomfortable parallels with Turkey's own problems in the Kurdish southeast and with Middle Eastern neighbors.

A confluence of influences underlies the recent upsurge in Turkish nationalism, although as noted, this upsurge faces some countervailing tendencies. On balance, Turkish nationalism may now be a more potent force than political Islam, and with equally important implications for relations with the United States and the EU. The success of Turkey's Islamists at the local and national levels during the 1990s can be ascribed to many factors, of which the rise in religious sentiment may not have been the most significant. Economic populism and an efficient grass-roots party machinery also played a part.[5] In the period leading up to Refah's entry in a governing coalition, it was also very effective in articulating a nationalist message. This message has recently been taken up by an MHP that now seeks to portray itself as mainstream. It is echoed on the opposite end of the political spectrum by Bulent Ecevit's Democratic Left Party (DLP). DLP finished first in Turkey's 1999 elections, largely on the strength of Prime Minister Ecevit's own personality, untainted by corruption and strongly nationalist in tone. The traditional centrist parties—True Path (DYP) and Motherland (ANAP)—faired poorly in the elections, as did Refah's successor—the Virtue Party—when measured against previous results and preelection expectations. Overall, the 1999 elections were a triumph for Turkish nationalists of the left and the right.[6] Yet the postelection period has also seen significant improvement in relations with Greece and the EU, two areas where nationalist sentiment would normally act as a constraint.

The 1999 election results, and the formation of a new coalition embracing MHP, has produced an active debate over whether this party has definitively abandoned the violent extremism associated with MHP in the past. During the late 1970s, MHP under the leadership of Alparslan Turkes was linked to right-wing terrorism and political violence carried out by the Grey Wolves and others.[7] The youth wing of MHP has had a particularly violent reputation, a fact that takes on special significance given the high percentage of young voters opting for MHP in recent elections. In postelection pronouncements, Turkey's National Security Council identified the Grey Wolves and

---

[5]The socioeconomic explanation of Refah's strength is emphasized in many recent analyses. See, for example, Nilufer Narli, "The Rise of the Islamist Movement in Turkey," *Middle East Review of International Affairs*, Vol. 3, No. 3 (September 1999).

[6]1999 general election results gave the Democratic Left Party (DSP) 22 percent, Nationalist Action Party (MHP) 18 percent, Virtue Party 15 percent, Motherland (ANAP) 13.3 percent, and True Path (DYP) 12.5 percent. The Pro-Kurdish Party (HADEP) received some 4 percent of the overall vote, but did very well at the local level in the southeast. Similarly, Virtue did well enough at the local level to retain many key mayoral positions won in 1995.

[7]The Grey Wolves, the militaristic youth organization affiliated with MHP, played a major role in the political violence that swept Turkey in the 1970s. The group has kept a lower profile over the last decade.

related groups as "an increasing danger."[8]   Although ostensibly a secular party, MHP, like the center-right parties, has a religious wing, and is flexible on educational and cultural issues (e.g., the headscarf question) important to Turkey's Islamists. The party has benefited from Virtue's decline under pressure from the secular establishment and the courts.[9]

The postelection political scene in Turkey has several potentially important implications for Turkish foreign policy and relations with the United States. First, and most positively, the formation of a stable three-party coalition should allow Ankara to move on legislation and policy initiatives with relevance to Turkey's external relations. Social security reform, privatization, and intellectual property legislation now have a better prospect of moving forward. Both are linked to the longer-term outlook for the Turkish economy and opportunities for U.S. trade and investment. The new government may also have more freedom for maneuver on sensitive issues such as human rights, including the Kurdish question. Some evidence of this movement can be seen in comments by Foreign Minister Ismail Cem that Kurdish language broadcasts should be allowed, a statement that would have been unthinkable from a key government minister until very recently. Improvements in these areas could have a dramatic and salutary effect on relations with Europe as well as the United States. That said, the nationalist outlook of the current coalition suggests that Ankara will not be well-disposed toward international pressure on these issues; and increasing international (especially European) scrutiny is now more likely in the wake of the Helsinki summit.[10]

Second, growing nationalism is likely to reinforce existing trends in Turkey's external policy, and will support a more active, assertive,

---

[8]Kemal Balci, "MHP: Hard to Live with, Harder to Live Without," *Turkish Daily News*, April 27, 1999.

[9]This pressure is being redoubled in the wake of arrests and revelations surrounding "Turkish Hizbullah" in the winter of 1999–2000. See Ersel Aydinli, "Implications of Turkey's Anti-Hizbullah Operation," *PolicyWatch*, #439, Washington Institute for Near East Policy, February 9, 2000.

[10]The EU's political sanctions on Austria, imposed after the formation of a government including right-wing nationalists, suggest that Europe is becoming more critical and more willing to intervene in areas that could affect Turkey.

and sovereignty-conscious approach in key areas. Prime Minister Ecevit has consistently emphasized a "regionally based" foreign policy in which Ankara seeks to play a more active role in defense of its own interests in adjoining areas. In practice this has meant a more assertive policy toward Syria, Iran, Northern Iraq, the Aegean, and Cyprus.[11] Potentially, it could mean a more assertive policy in the Balkans, the Caucasus, and the Caspian, although Turkish policymakers have thus far pursued a very cautious, multilateral approach to these areas.

Third, the nationalist tendency can complicate Turkish relations with the United States, despite the growing importance of the bilateral relationship as seen from Ankara. Turkish sensitivities with regard to sovereignty issues will likely be the key concern. Turkish constitutional provisions do not allow for the permanent stationing of foreign military forces on Turkish territory. Yet, through various rotational arrangements and deployments sanctioned by the Turkish parliament (e.g., for Operations Provide Comfort and, more recently, Northern Watch) the United States has enjoyed what amounts to a standing airpower presence in Turkey. Since the Gulf War, access to Turkish facilities for non-NATO purposes has been closely measured against Turkish interests and, increasingly, public acceptance. More active nationalist sentiment does not preclude close cooperation with the United States in regional matters, including the use of Turkish facilities for contingencies in the Gulf, the Balkans, or elsewhere (as recent experience in Northern Iraq and Kosovo illustrates), but it does make cooperation less automatic and less predictable. It can also complicate relations on key issues such as policy toward Greece and Russia, where U.S. and Turkish approaches may diverge. Moreover, it suggests no real diminution in the long-standing Turkish sensitivity to arms-transfer issues in relations with Washington.

MHP's participation in government is unlikely to signal radical changes in Turkish foreign policy since, as noted earlier, nationalist sentiment has been a strong force in Turkish policy for some time. MHP holds the defense portfolio (a relatively weak actor in the Turkish system) but is otherwise not heavily represented in foreign poli-

---

[11]Bulent Ecevit is known for his particularly strong stance on the Cyprus issue, having approved the Turkish military intervention in Cyprus in 1974.

cymaking circles. That said, MHP views on external policy can have an important effect over time, especially in response to crises when public opinion is actively engaged. MHP's foreign policy statements have emphasized strengthening relations with the Turkic republics of Central Asia; a tough stance on Cyprus as a matter of "vital and strategic importance" for Turkey; and a critical, arm's-length approach to the EU. The party has been particularly vocal in relation to developments in Azerbaijan and Armenian-Azeri relations, and is likely to be a continuing factor in Ankara's relations with Baku. MHP has also stressed Turkey's responsibility to defend the interests of Turks abroad (e.g., in Germany), Turkish and Muslim communities in the Balkans, and Turkomans in the Middle East. In a manner reminiscent of Erbakan's forays during the period of Refah-led government, MHP's program notes the imperative of creating a "social, economic, scientific, and cultural union" in the Turkish world, viewing this as essential to peace and stability in Eurasia.[12] The MHP program also asserts that "a ring of pacts should be formed around Turkey," including the establishment of an ambitious "East Mediterranean Union" embracing Turkey, Israel, Jordan, Egypt, and "Palestine," and perhaps eventually Lebanon, Syria, and Saudi Arabia.[13] This idea, probably more rhetorical than substantive, is made even more curious by MHP's traditional coolness toward relations with Israel, and allegations of past anti-Semitism.[14]

MHP has been very clear on the central role of the Turkish military, and an extensive military modernization program, in ensuring that Turkey can play an active geopolitical role, noting the need for "transcontinental" as well as cross-border military capabilities. The MHP program is notably silent on the issue of relations with the United States, and makes no mention of prominent policy questions

---

[12]Cited in Sibel Utku, "MHP Foreign Policy: Turkish World and Cyprus, But What Else?" *Turkish Daily News*, April 27, 1999. The Erbakan legacy in this area is examined in Philip Robins, "Turkish Foreign Policy under Erbakan," *Survival*, Vol. 39, No. 2 (Summer 1997), pp. 82–100.

[13]Utku. The strength of MHP's nationalist sensitivities was clearly displayed after the August 1999 earthquake, when the MHP Health Minister, Osman Durmus, issued a series of statements reflecting the need for foreign assistance in highly chauvinistic terms. His comments drew a strongly negative reaction from the media and Turkish public opinion.

[14]A Surprise in Turkey," *Foreign Report*, No. 2542, May 6, 1999, p. 2.

such as relations with Syria and the future of the Baku-Ceyhan
pipeline. Overall, the MHP program envisions Turkey's emergence
as a "leader state" and stresses the protection of the national interest
as a guiding principle.[15]

TRADITIONAL VERSUS MODERN WORLDVIEWS

Beyond the rise of Turkish nationalism as a political force, the past
decade has seen the growth of a sharper division in Turkish society
between "traditional" and "modern" worldviews. This polarization
can be expressed partly, but not entirely, in terms of friction between
religious and secular outlooks. Refah and its successor, Virtue,
tapped this vein of traditionalism in Turkish society. The social and
economic strains caused by Turkey's changing demographics, with
the steady movement of population from the countryside to the
cities, have been part of this phenomenon.[16] Notions of "trickle-
down" secularism, for example, had a very different meaning when
Turkey's population was 14 million at the foundation of the Republic
(it is some 65 million today).[17] Migration to the major urban areas
has brought traditional Anatolian patterns of life and conservative
social attitudes into areas where a secular, "European" outlook has
flourished in recent decades. Notably, this is not simply a clash of
attitudes between "haves" and "have-nots." The ranks of the traditionally minded include many middle-class Turks, and even some
conservative members of the economic elite.[18] The headscarf issue,
as well as the debate over religious education, have been symbolic
battlegrounds in this competition of social outlooks, a competition

---

[15]Utku.

[16]By 1997, 65 percent of Turkey's population was urban. In 1945, urban dwellers were
some 25 percent of the population. *Turkey's Window of Opportunity: Demographic
Transition Process and Its Consequences,* Istanbul: TUSIAD, 1999, p. 21. On demographics as a force for change in Turkey, see also Andrew Mango, *Turkey: The Challenge of A New Role,* Westport, CT: Praeger, 1994, pp. 64–75.

[17]The author is grateful to Heath Lowry for this formulation. These issues are also
taken up in a review article by Andrew Mango, "Progress and Disorder: 75 Years of the
Turkish Republic," *Middle Eastern Studies,* Vol. 35, No. 3 (July 1999), pp. 156–177.

[18]Affluent, traditionally minded Anatolian businessmen have been among the leading
supporters of Islamic institutions and Islamist politics in Turkey. Traditional religious
orders—*tarikats*—operating in a semi-underground fashion, continue to play an important part in the social and economic life of the country.

that probably reached its peak at the time of Refah's forced departure from government. Although the outcome of the 1999 elections shifted the focus from religion to nationalism, traditionalism is far from a spent force. It is likely that nationalist movements, especially MHP, have thrived precisely because they bridge these disparate tendencies, and offer an attractive synthesis. Various "communal" organizations and identities—Alevi, Sunni, Kurdish, etc.—have been another beneficiary of the urbanization process.[19] Despite the varying fortunes of Islamic political parties, Islamic institutions remain a potent social and economic force, and their containment continues to represent one of the two principal security challenges identified by Turkey's National Security Council (alongside the fight against separatism).[20]

The competing visions of the "traditional" and the "modern" affect the way foreigners see Turkey.[21] The debate over Refah and the Islamist question in Turkey was responsible for a significant increase in attention to Turkey in Washington and in the international media. This growth in interest has endured even though the Refah issue has faded, sustained by the Öcalan affair, Kosovo, the disastrous earthquake of August 1999, and the more recent and positive developments in Turkish relations with Greece and the EU. U.S. observers, on the whole, have been more tolerant of Islamist politics (and less alarmist about religious expression) in Turkey than has been the case in Europe. Explanations for this include the more highly politicized nature of relations with Muslim communities in Europe and a more relaxed American approach to secularism. In Europe, especially in France, the notion of secularism (*laïcité*) is more restrictive and intimately linked to modernity. For many Europeans, the success of Islamist political parties in Turkey was interpreted as a retreat from the modern and a rejection of the European path. U.S. observers, in spite of—perhaps because of—the Iranian experience, have been less concerned about the internal implications of the Refah/Virtue phe-

---

[19] *Turkey's Window of Opportunity*, p. 25.

[20] Even in the context of earthquake-relief efforts, Ankara has attempted to limit the role of Islamic groups. Stephen Kinzer, "Turkey Blocking Muslim Aid to Quake Victims," *New York Times*, August 27, 1999, p. 3.

[21] These contrasts have formed the basis for many descriptions of the Turkish scene. For a recent example, see Nicole and Hugh Pope, *Turkey Unveiled: A History of Modern Turkey*, Woodstock, NY: Overlook, 1997.

nomenon, preferring to focus on the foreign policy consequences of Islamic politics in Turkey.

One important area in which the distinction between traditionalists and modernists is less clear concerns the approach to democratization, human rights, and minority issues. Here, the religious and (some) nationalist elements have adopted a reformist attitude, in part because a relaxation of existing restrictions gives these groups greater room for maneuver. They are joined in this approach by reformist intellectuals and influential elements in the business community whose interest in change is aimed at the development of a more stable, modern society.[22] Closer relations with the EU are interpreted as supporting this reformist tendency.

The Turkish military and the bureaucracy have been more resistant to reforms, including economic reforms, which they view as threatening to the security, integrity, and welfare of the state. Ironically, these two institutions have been pillars of the modern Republic and staunch supporters of an Atatürkist vision of modernity. As many Turks will now admit, the economic dimension of this vision, with its emphasis on statism and centralization, no longer looks very modern in light of liberalization and decentralization elsewhere. The evolution of the Turkish debate on these issues will shape the outlook for Turkey in the 21st century, as well as the continued viability of U.S. and European views of Turkey as a developmental "model."

EMERGENCE OF A DYNAMIC PRIVATE SECTOR

The rapid, if uneven, economic growth of the last decade has been supported by the emergence of a dynamic and increasingly influential Turkish private sector.[23] The effects of this change have been most obvious in the commercial arena, but the changing balance between private organizations and the state is being felt across Turkish society. Many Turks are increasingly uncomfortable with the tradi-

---

[22]The Turkish Industrialists' and Businessmen's Association (TUSIAD) has been an active and outspoken "elite" advocate for reform, including political approaches to the issue of Kurdish rights.

[23]The Turkish economy averaged over 5 percent growth since 1980, the highest average in the Organization for Economic Cooperation and Development (OECD).

tional, dominant role of state institutions. This discomfort is reflected in declining public confidence in the competence of the state and a growing tendency to organize lives and enterprises without any reference to the state. A prominent Turkish businessman, active in politics, has termed this tendency a "darker version of the Italian model": a dynamic private sector (and more broadly, "civil society") tending to its own business and increasingly frustrated by the tendency of Turkish democracy and administration to lag behind.[24] It is a "darker" version of a trend visible elsewhere in southern Europe and the Mediterranean because the Turkish state has numerous enemies, including some violent ones (e.g., the PKK and extremists on the secular right, the religious right, and the left). The disorganized response of the Turkish administration to the devastating earthquake of August 1999 gave considerable impetus to this criticism of the state, although it has not produced the pressure for dramatic change that was widely anticipated at the time.

The state remains a leading actor in the Turkish economy and society as a whole.[25] But the balance is changing, with several important implications for bilateral relations with the United States. First, high growth rates, a large potential market, the proliferation of private business partners, and the need for investment in key sectors (e.g., energy) should make Turkey a more attractive economic partner for the United States. The United States has for some time treated Turkey as a "big emerging market," and bilateral trade has grown steadily since the mid-1980s.[26] That said, and with some exceptions such as power generation, U.S. and other foreign investment in Turkey has consistently fallen short of expectations. Large deficits, high inflation, lack of structural reform, halfhearted privatization efforts, and the deepening problem of the illegal sector have con-

---

[24]See Stephen Kinzer, "Businesses Pressing a Reluctant Turkey on Democracy Issues," *New York Times*, March 23, 1997.

[25]State-owned enterprises accounted for some 10 percent of GNP in the first half of the 1990s. These enterprises have come under pressure in recent years from International Monetary Fund (IMF)-led monitoring, privatization initiatives, and some outright closures. See OECD, *Turkey: Economic Survey*, 1995–96.

[26]The United States has a favorable trade balance with Turkey, and the volume of trade has more than tripled since 1980, increasing from $1.6 billion in 1985 to $3.4 billion in 1998. See Yilmaz Arguden, "Is Uncle Sam Making the Most of Turkey?" *Private View* (Istanbul), Spring 1999, available on-line only, solvista@binternet.com.

tributed to this lackluster performance. Political instability and turmoil in Ankara's relations with the EU have also played a role. Nonetheless, the economic dimension of Turkey's external relations has grown enormously in importance over the past decade, most obviously in relations with Russia and Europe, but also in relations with the United States. Economic and "geo-economic" issues such as energy investment, Caspian oil routes, Balkan reconstruction, and cooperation on international crime, are acquiring greater importance, and offer an opportunity to diversify the "security-heavy" bilateral agenda.

Second, the rise of the Turkish private sector is influencing the constellation of actors within Turkey on policy questions of concern to the United States, from regional trade to defense procurement, and not least, the Kurdish issue.[27] Broadly, leading commercial power centers in Turkey include the military (with a large stake in the Turkish economy); secular holding companies; Islamist business interests; the unions (in decline but still influential, especially on welfare and privatization issues); and the very substantial illegal sector (drug trafficking, money laundering, etc.).[28] Private-sector organizations, notably the Turkish Industrialists' and Businessmen's Association (TUSIAD), representing a constellation of the most prominent Turkish holding companies, have begun to articulate policy interests in a modern, institutionalized manner.[29] At the same time, these organizations are emerging as more important and influential interlocutors for the United States on strategic issues— another useful opportunity for diversification in bilateral relations.

Dynamism in the private sector is also having an important effect on mobility in Turkish society. Whereas Turks have traditionally seen state service (above all, the military) as the path to social and profes-

---

[27]On the relationship between the private sector and the state in Turkey, see Ayse Bugra, *State and Business in Modern Turkey: A Comparative Study*, Albany, NY: State University of New York Press, 1994.

[28]The role of these power centers is discussed in an analysis of the Turkish private sector by Ian Lesser and Michele Zanini summarized in Gregory F. Treverton, et al., *Commercial Power Centers in Emerging Markets*, Santa Monica, CA.: RAND, MR-950, 1998.

[29]TUSIAD is also a leading sponsor of research and analysis on public policy matters concerning Turkey. See, for example, the recently published TUSIAD report, *Turkey's Window of Opportunity.*

sional advancement, younger generations now look to the private sector.[30] To the extent that this trend continues, it suggests that the role of the military in Turkish society may be changing, and that new elites may have a very different background and worldview. In a bilateral relationship that has stressed military-to-military ties, and has focused on security issues in preference to economic and other links, changes along these lines could have important implications for U.S. engagement in Turkey. It also points to the importance for Western interlocutors of identifying new and emerging elites outside traditional state-centered institutions.

Third, the rise of the private sector has important implications for Turkey's future regional role and the potential for bilateral cooperation in regional stability and development. Turkish entrepreneurs have played a leading role in the burgeoning economic relationship between Turkey and Russia (now Ankara's leading trade partner). In the Arab Middle East, where Turkey's official relationships have often been difficult, the private sector has been an active player. Turkish influence in the Caucasus and Central Asia has been advanced considerably by the role of Turkish companies and foundations. In the Balkans, where economic reconstruction is high on the international agenda, and closely linked to regional security, the Turkish private sector is involved. Finally, it is worth noting that leading actors on the Turkish commercial scene have been among the most active in attempts to improve Turkish-Greek relations, including joint ventures in the Balkans and elsewhere.[31] The role of the private sector is thus likely to have a considerable influence on Turkish policy in regions where Washington and Ankara have a shared stake.

A MORE STABLE INTERNAL ENVIRONMENT?

In sum, Turkish society, politics, and economy are in a state of considerable flux. Recent trends have yielded a more stable domestic

---

[30]Ties between the military and the private sector remain important, however, especially for the larger holding companies, where retired general officers are frequently part of senior management.

[31]Among the more imaginative of these joint ventures is a plan for a Greek-Turkish energy generation plant that would export electricity to Turkey and perhaps elsewhere in the Balkans.

scene, but with many residual and unresolved sources of tension. Turkey's much vaunted identity crisis, both internal and external, has hardly been resolved. What is clear is that today's Turkey is an increasingly diverse society in terms of policy perceptions and outlooks. Overall, this diversity and the sheer dynamism of the Turkish debate points in the direction of a more modern and, broadly, more "Western" Turkey. It is a Turkey that is capable of having its own vibrant debate about what the country's many new international opportunities, including the prospect of deeper integration with Europe, really mean.

Many of the key risks to stability and security, as Turks define them, are also internal. Although the United States and Europe have their own domestic challenges, including some in the security realm, the focus on internal security is no longer the norm in the West as a whole, and points to a critical area of difference between Turkey and its Western partners. It can also be the source of enduring U.S., and especially European, ambivalence in relations with Ankara. Ideally, the processes of modernization and reform in Turkish society—supported by the opening of the European path—will close this important gap between Turkey and the West in the coming decades. Looking ahead, the key trends of nationalism, changing state and private-sector roles, and the tension between modern and traditional outlooks (a large part of the identity question) will be important drivers of Turkey's external role and Ankara's relations with Western allies.

Chapter Three

TURKISH FOREIGN AND SECURITY POLICY: NEW DIMENSIONS AND NEW CHALLENGES

F. Stephen Larrabee

Turkey's international role and posture have been profoundly affected by the end of the Cold War. The collapse of communism in Eastern Europe and the Soviet Union forced Turkey to redefine and reshape its foreign policy in important ways. Initially many Turks feared that the end of the Cold War would diminish Turkey's strategic importance. These fears, however, proved to be unfounded. Turkey's strategic importance has increased, not decreased, as a result of the end of the Cold War.

In the last decade, moreover, Turkey has become a more self-confident and assertive actor and has demonstrated a willingness to act unilaterally if necessary. The most striking example of this trend was Turkey's confrontation with Syria in October 1998 over Baghdad's support of the Kurdistan Workers Party (PKK). But there are other recent examples, including Ankara's threat to use force to prevent the deployment of the SS-300 missiles by the Greek Cypriot government and its daring capture of PKK leader Abdullah Öcalan in Kenya in February 1999. Indeed, Öcalan's capture has significantly contributed to this new mood of self-confidence.

Turkish domestic politics have also been characterized by a more vigorous nationalism lately. The current coalition, comprising of Prime Minister Bulent Ecevit's Democratic Left Party (DLP) and the right-wing Nationalist Action Party (MPH), reflects this new nationalist orientation. Both parties rode to power on a tide of rising nationalism, fueled in part by the struggle against the PKK as well as

Turkey's perceived rejection by Europe. As Alan Makovsky has noted, it is this more assertive, more self-confident mood that both Ecevit and MHP leader Devlet Bahceli exploited and that is increasingly reflected in Turkish policy on a number of international issues.[1]

In short, the old paradigm that characterized Turkey's relations with the West during the Cold War is no longer valid. Turkey's foreign policy interests are beginning to evolve in new and important ways. This process of rethinking and redefinition of Turkish interests could have significant consequences over the long run for Turkey's foreign policy orientation and, in particular, for its relations with the West.

THE RUSSIAN FACTOR

The new dynamics unleashed by the end of the Cold War have not only expanded Turkey's foreign policy horizons but have also led to an important shift in Turkish security perceptions. During the Cold War the main threat to Turkish security came from the Soviet Union. Today, by contrast, Turkey sees the main threat to its security from Iraq and Syria (and to a lesser extent Iran). Russia remains an important residual concern but it does not represent the type of existential threat that the Soviet Union did.

Still, Russia figures more prominently in Turkish security concerns than it does in those of most NATO members. The Ottoman Empire fought 13 wars with czarist Russia, most of which it lost. This has instilled in Turks a healthy respect for Russian power and Russia's ability to bounce back, even if it is weak at the moment. More fundamentally, Russian and Turkish political agendas clash, particularly in Central Asia and the Caucasus (see below). As a consequence, Turkey is both more concerned about containing Russian power as well as more eager to avoid antagonizing Russia than are most other NATO allies.

Moreover, Turkish-Russian relations remain burdened by differences over several specific issues:

---

[1]See Alan Makovsky, "Turkey's Nationalist Moment,"
The Washington Quarterly, Vol. 22, No. 4 (Autumn 1999), pp. 159–166.

Cyprus

The Russian sale of S-300 missiles to the (Greek) Republic of Cyprus badly strained relations between Ankara and Moscow and created a major crisis in the Eastern Mediterranean. While the crisis was later defused when Cyprus agreed to deploy the missiles on Crete rather than on the Cypriot mainland, Russia's role in the crisis reinforced Turkish concerns about Russia's broader political ambitions in the region.

The Kurdish Issue

Russia's attitude toward the Kurdish insurrection has been ambivalent at best. While Moscow has refrained from directly stoking the fires of Kurdish nationalism, it has allowed Kurdish nationalist groups to openly agitate and hold meetings on Russian soil.[2] In addition, it briefly gave sanctuary to PKK leader Abdullah Öcalan, who is considered by the Turkish government to be a terrorist, after his expulsion from Syria. These actions have deepened Turkish suspicions about Moscow's policy goals while at the same time making Turkey wary of antagonizing Russia, for fear that Moscow could step up its support for Kurdish separatists.

Conventional Forces in Europe (CFE)

Turkey has been concerned about the buildup of Russian forces in the Southern Caucasus in violation of the CFE Treaty. Under U.S. pressure, Ankara agreed to the compromise worked out at the First Review Conference in Vienna in May 1996, which gave Russia an additional three years to comply with the flank limitations in the treaty. However, Ankara is likely to resist further efforts to reduce these limits or eliminate them entirely, as Moscow wants. This could

---

[2]In November 1994, Moscow permitted the establishment of a Confederation of Kurdish Organizations of the Commonwealth of Independent States (CIS). At its opening session, posters of PKK leader Abdullah Öcalan bedecked the Congress Hall and some representatives openly called upon delegates to assist the PKK. In October 1995, the third session of the Kurdish "parliament in exile" convened in a building attached to the Russian Duma, with several Duma deputies in attendance. See Malik Mufti, "Daring and Caution in Turkish Foreign Policy," *Middle East Journal*, Vol. 52, No. 1 (Winter 1998), p. 38.

put Turkey at odds with some of its Western allies, including the United States, who may be more inclined to compromise in order to achieve Russian cooperation on other issues, particularly the Strategic Arms Reduction Talks (START).

Chechnya

Turkish sympathy for the Chechens has been a source of friction in relations with Russia. However, official Turkish policy toward Chechnya has been cautious. The Turkish government had been reluctant to openly support the Chechen cause because of its own problems with Kurdish separatism. Instead it has regarded Chechnya largely as a Russian "internal affair."[3] At the same time, Turkish officials are worried that Russia's effort to subdue the rebels in Chechnya could be a prelude to an attempt by Russia to seek to bring the whole of the Caucasus—including Georgia and Azerbaijan—under its control. Such an effort would bring Russia's military presence closer to Turkey's border and undercut Turkish attempts to expand its influence in the Caucasus. The refugee outflow from Chechnya has also caused difficulties for Turkey, which has been forced to accept thousands of Chechen refugees.

Differences over these issues have tended to exacerbate the broader political rivalry and struggle for influence in the Caucasus and Central Asia. At the same time, they have made Turkey cautious about provoking Russia. Turkey does not want to see a strengthening of Russian influence in the Caucasus, which is becoming an area of increasing strategic importance for Turkey. One of the main reasons for Turkey's initial lack of enthusiasm for NATO enlargement, for instance, was Ankara's fear that this would provoke Moscow to try to expand its military presence in the Caucasus.

---

[3]During his trip to Russia in late 1999, Turkish Prime Minister Bulent Ecevit referred to Chechnya as a Russian "internal affair"—a statement that was widely criticized by many Turks. Moreover, Turkish criticism of Russia's policy toward Chechnya at the Organization for Security and Cooperation in Europe (OSCE) summit in Istanbul in November 1999 was much more muted than that of many other Western countries who had far weaker interests in Chechnya. See Stephen Kinzer, "Turkey Faces Quandary on Relations by Friends," *New York Times*, November 28, 1999.

Turkey also has a strong economic stake in maintaining good relations with Moscow. Russia is Turkey's second largest trade partner behind Germany and its main supplier of natural gas. In addition, a flourishing "suitcase trade" between Turkey and Russia exists. While this trade has declined recently, it accounts for an important part of the unofficial Turkish economy. Thus, Ankara has a strong economic incentive to keep relations with Russia on an even keel.

At the same time, Turkey has sought to strengthen ties to other regional actors around the Black Sea, particularly Ukraine. Turkey and Ukraine share a number of common interests: both countries are concerned about Russia's efforts to increase its influence in the Caucasus and the Commonwealth of Independent States (CIS). Economic cooperation, especially in the energy sector, has recently been intensified. In June 1997, the two countries signed an agreement for the construction of a pipeline between the port of Ceyhan on Turkey's Mediterranean coast and its Black Sea port of Samsun. The pipeline could help Ukraine reduce its dependence on Russian oil.

Military cooperation has also been stepped up. During the visit of then Turkish Prime Minister Yilmaz to Ukraine in February 1998, the two countries agreed to upgrade their relationship and to increase cooperation in the energy and security field.[4] This evolving "strategic partnership" between Turkey and Ukraine could become an important geopolitical factor in the Black Sea area in the future. But Turkey is likely to be careful not to let its cooperation with Ukraine develop to the point that it becomes a major irritant in relations with Russia.

CENTRAL ASIA AND THE CAUCASUS

The end of the Cold War has also presented new opportunities and options in Central Asia and the Caucasus.[5] With the collapse of the former Soviet Union, a whole new "Turkish world" has opened up

---

[4]"Turkey and Ukraine Advancing Toward an Extensive Partnership," *Turkish Daily News*, February 17, 1998.

[5]For a comprehensive discussion, see Graham E. Fuller, *Turkey Faces East: New Orientations Toward the Middle East and Old Soviet Union*, Santa Monica, CA: RAND, R-4234-AF/A, 1992.

that was previously closed to Turkish policy. While Turkey has been relatively cautious about exploiting these possibilities, the reemergence of Central Asia and the Caucasus has given a new geopolitical dimension to Turkish policy that did not exist earlier. It has also prompted an internal debate in Turkey about Turkish national interests that could have important implications for Turkish policy over the long run, especially if pro-Islamic or nationalist forces in Turkey gain greater strength.[6]

At the same time, the energy issue has given Turkish interest in Central Asia and the Caucasus a sharper focus.[7] The Caspian region is a major source of gas and oil that Turkey needs to meet its increasing domestic energy requirements. Ankara is particularly interested in the construction of a pipeline to carry Caspian oil from Baku in Azerbaijan to the port of Ceyhan on Turkey's Mediterranean coast. This would not only help ensure Turkey's growing domestic energy needs but also increase its political influence in the region.

In addition to its strong support for the construction of the Baku-Ceyhan pipeline, Ankara is also interested in the construction of a gas pipeline between Turkmenistan and Turkey. The line will provide the first viable export route out of Turkmenistan that circumvents Russia and will help to ensure Turkmenistan's energy independence as well as its viability as an independent state. The Turkmenistan-Turkey pipeline would parallel the Baku-Ceyhan oil pipeline and could sideline alternative routes such as the Russian "Blue Stream" project—dubbed "Blue Dream" by critics—to transport natural gas to Turkey underneath the Black Sea.

The energy issue has given the old historical rivalry between Turkey and Russia a sharper geopolitical—and economic—focus. Increasingly Russia has come to see Turkey as the major rival for influence in Central Asia and the Caspian region. In some ways the 19th century "Great Game" is being replayed in a new geopolitical context, with oil

---

[6]See Ola Tunander, "A New Ottoman Empire?" *Security Dialogue*, Vol. 26, No. 4, pp. 413–426.

[7]For a detailed discussion of the Caspian energy issue, see Rosemarie Forsythe, "The Politics of Oil in the Caucasus and Central Asia," *Adelphi Paper*, No. 300, London: International Institute for Strategic Studies, May 1996.

and pipelines replacing the railroads as the main means of extending political influence.[8]

In the initial period after the collapse of the Soviet Union, Turkey, sparked by euphoric expectations that it could become the unofficial leader of a Pan-Turkic community, sought to expand its ties to the countries of Central Asia.[9] Turkey opened cultural centers and Turkic schools in most of the Central Asian states and provided training and technical assistance for thousands of Central Asian students. Ankara also expanded its television broadcasts in an effort to extend its cultural influence in Central Asia.

However, Turkey's effort to expand its ties in Central Asia has met with mixed results. The reasons for Turkey's spotty record are varied:

- First, Turkey overestimated the cultural and linguistic affinity with the new independent states of Central Asia.

- Second, Turkey's own domestic problems—specifically, the growth of Kurdish separatism and the challenge posed by the rise of Islamic forces in Turkish politics—diverted Turkish attention from the region.

- Third, Turkey was preoccupied by other, more pressing security concerns, including threats from Syria and Iraq; instability in the Balkans; and, until recently, the deterioration of relations with Greece over Cyprus and the Aegean.

- Fourth, Turkey lacked the economic means to provide the type of large-scale economic assistance and investment that the states in the region need and want.

---

[8]See Ariel Cohen, "The 'New Great Game': Pipeline Politics in Eurasia," *Eurasian Studies*, Vol. 3, No. 1 (Spring 1996), pp. 2–15. Also, Michael P. Croissant, "Oil and Russian Imperialism in the Transcaucasus," ibid., pp. 16–25. On the 19th-century struggle for influence in Central Asia and the Caucasus, see in particular Peter Hopkirk, *The Great Game*, New York: Kodansha International, 1990.

[9]For a good discussion of Turkish policy in this early period, see Philip Robins, "Between Sentiment and Self-Interest: Turkey's Policy Toward Azerbaijan and the Central Asian States," *Middle East Journal*, Vol. 47, No. 4 (Autumn 1993), pp. 593–610. Also, Gareth Winrow, *Turkey in Post-Soviet Central Asia*, London: Royal Institute of International Affairs, 1995; and Richard Sokolsky and Tanya Charlick-Paley, *NATO and Caspian Security: A Mission Too Far?*, Santa Monica, CA: RAND, MR-1074, 1999, pp. 40–44.

- Fifth, Turkey's cultural arrogance and pretensions to become the leader of the Pan-Turkic movement in Central Asia offended some Central Asian governments. Having just emancipated themselves from Soviet rule, these states were not about to exchange one form of domination for another.

These factors have dampened Turkey's initial high expectations about the prospects for a rapid expansion of Turkish influence in Central Asia in the near future. Turkey has by no means given up its aspirations to play an important role in the region. However, today there is a more sober and realistic understanding of the difficulties involved and the length of time that the process may take.

THE CAUCASUS

While Turkey's relations with Central Asia have witnessed a slowdown since the mid-1990s, Ankara has strengthened its position in the Caucasus, which has emerged as a region of growing strategic interest and importance for Turkey. Relations with Georgia have intensified, especially in the military field. In March 1999, Turkey and Georgia signed an agreement on military assistance and cooperation.[10] This military assistance, while limited, is part of a broader effort by Georgia to strengthen its independence and ties to the West, including NATO.

Turkey has also strengthened ties to Azerbaijan and strongly backed Baku in its struggle with Armenia over Nagorno-Karabakh. Turkey has been especially keen to obtain Azerbaijan's support for the construction of the Baku-Ceyhan pipeline, which it regards as an important vehicle for solving its growing energy needs in the coming decade as well as expanding its political and economic influence in the Caspian region.

Georgia and Azerbaijan both share Turkey's concerns about Russia's hegemonic aspirations in the Caucasus. With Turkish (and U.S.) assistance, both countries have adopted an increasingly pro-Western

---

[10]The five-year agreement envisages the construction in Georgia of military training centers in Kodori and Gori and a shooting range outside Tbilisi. See *Jamestown Monitor*, Vol. V, No. 45, March 5, 1999.

policy in the last several years and intensified their ties to NATO. Georgian President Eduard Shevardnadze has predicted that Georgia will be "knocking on NATO'S door" within five years,[11] while in December 1999 Azerbaijan's Foreign Minister Vilayet Guliev said that Azerbaijan intended to apply for "aspirant status in NATO." Units from Georgia and Azerbaijan are also participating in the Kosovo Force (KFOR) as part of a Turkish battalion.

Turkey and Georgia also launched a joint initiative to create a "South Caucasus Stability Pact." The proposal, which was made during Turkish President Suleyman Demirel's visit to Tbilisi in January 2000, would include Armenia, Azerbaijan, and Georgia as well as Turkey, Russia (and possibly Iran), the United States, the European Union (EU), and the Organization for Security and Cooperation in Europe (OSCE).[12] The International Monetary Fund (IMF) and World Bank would be asked to underwrite reconstruction aid for the region. The initiative, however, would not include Chechnya and the Northern Caucasus.

The pact is designed to increase Turkey's profile in the region as well as enhance Western involvement in the area. By including other Western powers as well as Russia, Turkey is, in effect, seeking to legitimize Western involvement in the area as well as implicitly asking Russia to view the region as an area of international cooperation rather than its own backyard. The proposal has the support of Azerbaijan as well as key Western governments, including the United States.

However, Turkey's ability to expand its influence in the Caucasus and Caspian region faces important constraints. The first is Russia's political ambitions and presence in the region. Russia has an extensive military presence in Armenia and also has access to four bases in Georgia. While Russia agreed at the OSCE summit in Istanbul (November 18–19, 1999) to close the bases at Vaziani and Gudauta by 2001, it still retains two other bases at Batumi and Akhalkati. Moreover, the conflict in Chechnya has increased Georgia's strategic importance in Russian eyes.

---

[11]See Andrew Jack and David Stern, "Georgia Plans to Seek NATO Membership," *Financial Times*, October 25, 1999.

[12]*Jamestown Monitor*, Vol. VI, No. 12, January 18, 2000.

In addition, Azerbaijan's political future remains uncertain. President Heydar Aliev has been highly successful in playing different internal factions in Azerbaijan off one another and in blocking Moscow's efforts to gain a military foothold in Azerbaijan. However, Aliev is 77 and in poor health. Turkish officials worry that his departure could spark an internal struggle for power and weaken Azerbaijan's current pro-Western orientation.

Turkey's poor relations with Armenia pose a third obstacle to an expansion of Turkey's influence in the Caucasus. Recently there have been small signs of a thaw in relations. But any far-reaching breakthrough in relations is only likely after a settlement of the Nagorno-Karabakh conflict. Such a settlement would allow Armenia to reduce its dependence on Russia and open up prospects for improving Turkish-Armenian relations.

Turkey's ability to achieve its broader objectives in the Caucasus and Caspian region will also heavily depend on the fate of the Baku-Ceyhan pipeline. Turkey has pinned its hopes for playing a major political role in the Caucasus and Central Asia on the construction of the pipeline, which it sees as the linchpin of its Central Asian and Caspian strategy. However, the Baku-Ceyhan pipeline has been plagued by delays and financing problems and it is unclear whether it will ever be built. Because the route is more expensive than other routes, Turkey has had problems attracting commercial backing for the project.

Turkey's campaign to obtain the support of Western oil companies for the construction of the Baku-Ceyhan pipeline received an important boost in November 1999 when BP-Amoco issued a statement supporting the pipeline after previously expressing doubts about its viability.[13] A framework agreement was signed by Turkey, Georgia, Azerbaijan, and Kazakhstan at the OSCE summit in Istanbul.[14] The inclusion of Kazakhstan considerably boosts the pipeline's economic viability. But Western oil companies remain concerned about the

---

[13]Leyla Boulton, "Deal Close on Financing Baku-Ceyhan Pipeline," *Financial Times*, October 22, 1999. Also Leyla Boulton, "Turkey and BP-AMOCO Step up Talks," ibid., October 26, 1999.

[14]Stephen Kinzer, "4 Nations in Caspian Sign Oil Pipeline Accord that Favors the West," *New York Times*, November 19, 1999.

commercial viability of the project.[15] To allay these concerns Turkey has agreed to guarantee any cost overruns above $1.4 billion for its part of the pipeline. However, the oil companies are likely to want to see additional alternative financing from other organizations such as the World Bank before they agree to take part.

In addition, the Baku-Ceyhan project could be affected by political changes in the Middle East. The United States has lobbied hard to exclude Iran from consideration as a transit route for Caspian oil. However, a thaw in U.S.-Iranian relations could open up prospects for shipping Caspian oil through Iran, a route that is favored by many Western companies because it would be cheaper. This would significantly reduce the interest of Western investors in the Baku-Ceyhan route.

Construction of a trans-Balkan pipeline could also affect prospects for the Baku-Ceyhan route. In June 1999, the U.S. Trade and Development Agency (TDA) announced a grant to Bulgaria to carry out a feasibility study for a pipeline across the Balkans. Under this scheme, Caspian oil would be shipped by tanker from the ports of Supsa in Georgia and Novorossiysk in Russia across the Black Sea to Bulgaria and then would be transported by pipeline across Macedonia and Albania. This route would be much cheaper than the Baku-Ceyhan route.[16]

THE MIDDLE EAST

Since the end of the Cold War, Turkey has also become a more important regional actor in the Middle East. The Gulf War was an important turning point in Turkey's involvement in the Middle East. Against the advice of most of his advisors, President Özal squarely sided with the United States in the war, allowing the United States to fly sorties against Iraq from Turkish bases. Turkey also shut down the Kirkuk-Yumurtalik pipeline as part of the effort to impose sanctions against Iraq.

---

[15]Jane Perlez, "U.S. Deal on the Caspian Still Faces Problems with the Bottom Line," *New York Times*, November 21, 1999.

[16]The cost for the Balkan route is estimated to be between $800 million and $1 billion, whereas cost estimates for Baku-Ceyhan range from $2.4 billion to $4 billion.

Özal's action was an important departure from Turkey's traditional policy of avoiding deep involvement in Middle Eastern affairs and provoked strong opposition, especially from the Turkish military.[17] At the same time, it initiated a new period of greater activism in Turkish policy toward the Middle East, which has intensified visibly since the mid-1990s. This more active policy contrasts markedly with the more passive approach that characterized Turkish policy before the Gulf War.

Iraq poses a difficult dilemma for Turkey. Turkish officials have no love for Saddam Hussein and they consider him to be a brutal dictator. At the same time, they have strong reservations about the wisdom of U.S. policy. They fear that U.S. efforts to topple Saddam could destabilize Iraq and lead to the creation of an independent Kurdish state on Turkey's border. They have looked askance, in particular, at U.S. efforts to promote a reconciliation between the warring Kurdish factions in northern Iraq.

Economic interests heavily influence Turkish policy toward Iraq. Before the imposition of UN sanctions, Iraq was Turkey's third largest trade partner and its largest oil supplier. Turkey would like to see this trade restored. Thus, Ankara favors a lifting of the UN sanctions against Iraq and an end to Iraq's economic isolation. Indeed, on many issues related to Iraq (and Iran), Turkish policy is much closer to European policy than it is to U.S. policy.

Turkey's relations with Syria have been strained by several issues: Syrian claims on the province of Hatay, which was ceded to Turkey by the colonial French authorities in Syria in 1939; Syrian demands for a more equitable sharing of the water resources of the Tigris and Euphrates rivers; and especially Syria's support for the PKK, which has led to tensions in relations between Ankara and Baghdad. One of the prime motivations behind Turkey's growing defense ties with Israel (see below) has been Turkey's desire to put pressure on Syria to halt its support of the PKK.

The tie to Israel has strengthened Turkey's hand diplomatically and was instrumental in Ankara's decision to force a showdown with

---

[17]The Turkish Chief of Staff, Necip Torumtay, resigned in protest over Özal's policy. So did Foreign Minister Ali Bozer.

Syria in the fall of 1998. In October 1998, frustrated by the lack of success of its repeated diplomatic efforts to get Syria to cease its support for the PKK, Turkey threatened to take military action against Syria if it did not halt its support for the Kurdish rebels.[18] Faced with the prospect of possible Turkish military action and military defeat, Syria backed down. Under an agreement signed in the Turkish city of Adana on October 20, 1998, the Syrian government agreed to cease all support for the PKK; expel PKK leader Abdullah Öcalan from Syria where he had taken refuge in the early 1980s; and expand cooperation with Turkey against the PKK.

Since then, Turkish-Syrian relations have undergone a visible thaw. PKK attacks from Syria have virtually ceased and a rudimentary monitoring system has been set up. It would be premature, however, to conclude that Turkish-Syrian relations have been permanently normalized. Syria appears to be trying to turn its momentary defeat into victory by insisting on a reciprocal gesture from Turkey on the water issue to normalize relations between the two countries. Moreover, it remains to be seen whether Syria will fully comply with the provisions of the Adana agreement, especially those regarding inspections.

Turkish relations with Iran have witnessed ups and downs over the last decade. Turkish policymakers, especially the Turkish military, remain wary of Iran because of the fundamentalist character of the current Iranian regime and its support for international terrorism. The Turkish military's crackdown against Islamic fundamentalism, moreover, has increased its sensitivity about Iran's influence and involvement in Turkish domestic politics. However, Turkey needs Iran's cooperation to curb the activities of the Kurdish guerrillas in Southeast Turkey, who often use Iranian territory as a sanctuary. Thus, Turkey has been careful not to let differences over other issues inflame its relations with Iran too badly.

Turkey's growing energy needs also give Ankara a strong incentive to maintain good economic ties to Iran, which is second only to Russia in the world's largest gas reserves. Turkey's annual gas needs of 8

---

[18]For a detailed discussion of the October 1998 crisis, see Mahmut Bali Aykan, "The Turkish-Syrian Crisis of October 1998: A Turkish View," *Middle East Policy*, Vol. VI, No. 4 (June 1999), pp. 174–191.

million cubic meters are expected to increase to 30 billion cubic me ters by the year 2005 and to reach 40 billion cubic meters by 2010.[19] Hence, for Turkey, increasing ties to Iran in the energy field makes good economic sense.

Relations have been troubled, however, by the delay in completing a gas pipeline for delivering Iranian natural gas. Tehran has completed its part of the pipeline, but Turkey's portion, which was due to be completed last year, remains unfinished. Turkish officials have said it will not be completed until 2001. Part of the reason for the delay is related to Turkey's economic problems caused by the August 1999 earthquake. But Ankara also appears to be going slow in deference to U.S. opposition to the pipeline, which Washington fears will strengthen Iran economically.

In addition, Turkey and Iran remain competitors for influence in the Caucasus and Central Asia. So far Turkey has had the upper hand because Iran has been isolated and preoccupied with its own internal problems. But a further thaw in U.S.-Iranian relations could open up prospects for Caspian oil to be transported via Iran and make Tehran a much more serious competitor for influence in Central Asia and the Caspian region.

The most important example of Turkey's new activism in the Middle East, however, has been its growing defense relationship with Israel. This effort has been highlighted by the signing of two military cooperation agreements with Tel Aviv in February and August 1996. The two agreements provide for joint air and naval exercises, allow access to port facilities, and permit the Israeli air force to conduct training exercises using Turkish airspace. They also call for increased exchanges of intelligence and stepped-up technological cooperation. Visits by high-level military officials have also increased.

The defense cooperation with Israel is seen by many Turks (especially the Turkish military) as a means of putting pressure on Syria and also of acquiring advanced military technology that Turkey might otherwise have trouble obtaining from Europe and the United States because of its human rights record and policy toward Cyprus. Some Turks also hope that the cooperation will enable Turkey to ex-

---

[19]See Cenk Bila, "Trade over Politics," *Turkish Probe,* November 8, 1996.

ploit the political clout of the Israeli lobby in Washington and counter the influence of the Greek and Armenian lobbies on Capitol Hill.

Turkish-Israeli defense cooperation has added an important new factor to the Middle East equation and given Turkey additional leverage in its relations with Syria. However, Turkey remains worried that the current Israeli-Syrian peace talks could adversely affect its interests.[20] Turkey has three concerns in particular: (1) that any peace deal not lead to a redeployment of Syrian troops along the Turkish-Syrian border; (2) that the United States retain Syria on its list of countries that sponsor state terrorism unless Syria halts its support for the PKK; and (3) that the peace negotiations not prejudice Turkey's negotiations with Syria over water.[21] Turkish officials are also concerned that a Middle East settlement could lead to a diminution of Israel's interest in Turkey. However, this seems unlikely to happen. The defense cooperation between Ankara and Israel has become too important for Israel to easily give it up.

Turkey has also quietly strengthened defense ties with Jordan. Turkey has had a military cooperation agreement with Jordan similar to the one with Israel since 1984. However, cooperation has intensified since the mid-1990s. In late 1996, Turkey and Jordan agreed to hold joint exercises and conduct bilateral training for their pilots in winter and desert conditions. Turkey also agreed to help Jordan strengthen its defense industries.[22] While this military cooperation remains relatively low-key, it has worried some Arab governments who fear that Jordan is being pulled into a strategic alliance with Turkey and Israel.

These developments highlight the degree to which Turkey has recently begun to play a more active—and assertive—role in the Middle East lately. However, there are important limits to Turkey's ability to expand its influence in the Middle East. First, Turkey is re-

---

[20]Burak Ege Begdil and Umit Enginsoy, "Turkey Uneasy with Israeli-Syrian Talks," *Defense News*, January 10, 2000. See also Alan Makovsky, "Syrian-Israeli Negotiations with Turkey," *Peacewatch*, December 17, 1999.

[21]See Haran Kazaz, "Water Talks Get Muddy," *Turkish Daily News*, January 15, 2000.

[22]Lale Sariibrahimoglu, "Turkey, Jordan Unlock Pilot Training Exchange," *Jane's Defense Weekly*, November 20, 1996.

garded with considerable distrust in the Arab world because of its imperial past. In addition, Turkey's strong attachment to secularism and its close ties to Washington are viewed with suspicion by many Arab countries.[23] Finally, the increasing strategic cooperation with Israel acts as an important obstacle to any far-reaching rapprochement with the Arab world.

THE BALKANS

Turkey has also pursued a more active policy in the Balkans since 1989. Historically Turkey has had a strong interest in the Balkans. From the 14th century until the end of the 19th century, the Ottoman Empire dominated the Balkan peninsula.[24] Gradually, however, the Ottomans were driven out of the Balkans. Greece was liberated from Ottoman rule in 1832. Romania and Bulgaria became independent states in 1878. In addition, Bosnia-Herzegovina was put under Austro-Hungarian administration in 1878 and formally annexed by Austria-Hungary in 1908. Albania and Macedonia were ceded in 1912 as a result of the First Balkan War.

With the establishment of the Turkish Republic in 1923, Turkey effectively abandoned its presence in the Balkans. While Turkey participated in four Balkan conferences in the interwar period, the main priority was the internal transformation of the new Turkish state. After World War II, Turkey's main foreign policy emphasis was on strengthening ties to the West, especially NATO and the United States. While Turkey did try to improve bilateral ties with some Balkan countries, on the whole the Balkans remained of secondary importance.

---

[23]The limits of Islamic solidarity were well illustrated by the ill-fated trip to Libya by then Turkish Prime Minister Necmettin Erbakan, the head of the Islamic Party Refah, in October 1996. Libyan leader Muammar-Qaddafi stunned Erbakan by unleashing a fierce anti-Turkish tirade, condemning Turkey for its ties to Israel and NATO and calling for an independent Kurdish state. See Stephen Kinzer, "Tirade by Qaddafi Stuns Turkey's Premier," *New York Times*, October 9, 1996.

[24]For a good discussion of the impact of Ottoman rule on the Balkans, see Maria Todorova, "The Ottoman Legacy in the Balkans," in L. Carl Brown, *Imperial Legacy, The Ottoman Imprint on the Balkans and Middle East,* New York: Columbia University Press, 1996, pp. 45–47.

Since the end of the Cold War, however, the Balkans have reemerged as an important focal point of Turkish foreign policy. Ties with Albania have been strengthened, especially in the military sphere. In July 1992, the two countries signed an agreement on military cooperation. Under the agreement, Turkey agreed to help modernize the Albanian army as well as help train Albanian officers.[25]

Ties with Macedonia have also been strengthened. Turkey was the first country after Bulgaria to recognize the new Macedonian state. Turkey is also helping to modernize Macedonia's armed forces. In July 1995, the two countries signed a military cooperation agreement providing for the exchange and training of military experts and joint military exercises. Turkey also agreed to give Macedonia 20 of its U.S.-made F-5s as part of its effort to assist the Macedonian army.[26]

The most far-reaching improvement, however, has occurred in relations with Bulgaria. During the Cold War, relations between Ankara and Sofia were marked by considerable hostility, in particular because of Bulgaria's mistreatment of the Turkish minority, which constitutes nearly 10 percent of the Bulgarian population. Relations deteriorated dramatically in 1989 when Bulgaria forced nearly 300,000 ethnic Turks to emigrate and confiscated their property.

However, relations have improved significantly since the collapse of the communist regime in Sofia in November 1989. The rights and property of the Turkish minority have been restored and more than half of the 320,000 ethnic Turks expelled in 1989 have returned to Bulgaria. In addition, several agreements on confidence-building measures have been signed which have helped to reduce threat perceptions and contributed to better mutual understanding. Indeed, Turkish-Bulgarian relations today are the best they have been since before World War II.

Turkey's more active policy in the Balkans initially caused some concern in Athens, which feared that Turkey was trying to create a

[25]See Louis Zanga, "Albania and Turkey Forge Closer Ties," *RFE/RL Research Report*, March 12, 1993, pp. 30–33.
[26]Umit Enginsoy, "Turkey to Give F-5s to Macedonia," *Defense News*, July 13, 1998.

"Muslim arc" on Greece's Northern border.[27] However, Turkey's policy in the Balkans has actually been relatively cautious. Turkey has not tried to "play the Muslim card," as some feared it might be tempted to do. Nor has it shown any inclination to take unilateral military action in the region. On the contrary, Turkey has gone out of its way to demonstrate its credentials as a good NATO ally. It participated in military operations in Bosnia and in both the Implementation Force (IFOR) and Stabilization Force (SFOR). It also contributed nearly one-tenth of the troops for Operation Alba (the Italian-led peacekeeping effort in Albania) and provided bases and aircraft for Operation Allied Force in Kosovo.

Turkey has also taken the lead in the establishment of a multinational peacekeeping force in the Balkans (the Southeast European Brigade, or SEEBRIG). The multinational force—comprising units from Turkey, Greece, Italy, Romania, Bulgaria, Macedonia, and Albania—has its headquarters in Plovdiv, Bulgaria. While it may take some time for the force to become militarily effective, the multilateral cooperation can help to promote greater regional trust and cooperation. Indeed, over the long term this may prove to be its most important function.

In short, while Turkey has pursued an active policy in the Balkans, this policy has remained very much within the Western mainstream. This has been true in Kosovo as well. Despite its strong historical, religious, and cultural ties to Albania, Turkey's approach to Kosovo has been very much in line with Western policy. Like other NATO members, Ankara favors maintaining Yugoslavia's territorial integrity and supports increased political autonomy—but not independence—for Kosovo, in part out of fear of setting a precedent on the Kurdish issue.

Turkey has a special interest in Kosovo because of the existence of a sizable Turkish minority there (about 30,000 to 40,000, mostly located around Prizren). The Turkish minority has appealed to Ankara for support in its struggle to maintain its cultural identity and have its own schools. However, these appeals present a dilemma for the government. The Turkish government cannot demand rights for the

---

[27]See Yannis Valinakis, *Greece's Balkan Policy and the "Macedonian Issue,"* Ebenhausen: Stiftung Wissenschaft und Politik, SWIP-2746, April 1992.

Turkish minority in Kosovo that it is unwilling to grant the Kurds in Turkey. Thus, Turkey is likely to avoid making the rights of the minority a high-profile issue in its Balkan policy.

RELATIONS WITH EUROPE

While Turkey's strategic horizons in other areas have broadened, its relations with Europe have become more difficult over the last decade. During the Cold War, Turkey was regarded as an important part of the Western security system. As a member of NATO, it served as a critical bulwark against any possible Soviet invasion of Europe, tying down some 24 Soviet divisions. Turkey's NATO membership reinforced Turkey's Western identification and accelerated the general process of Westernization of Turkish society that began in the 19th century under the Ottomans.

Turkey saw relations with the European Community (EC) as a natural complement to its relations with NATO. As a result of the 1963 Ankara agreement, Turkey became an associate member of the EC, with the expectation that someday it would eventually become a full member of the EC. Turkey's ties to the EC were enhanced in 1970 by the Additional Protocol, which foresaw the establishment of a Customs Union between Turkey and the EC. Relations with the EC, however, were always seen by Turkey in a broader political context— as part of the wider effort to Westernize Turkish society and complete the Atatürk revolution.

However, the end of the Cold War significantly changed the context for Turkish membership. Prior to the collapse of the Wall, Turkey's problems with the EC were primarily economic. Afterward, they broadened as the EC (later EU) began to put greater emphasis on political, social, and cultural factors. As Gulnur Aybet has noted, "Not only the parameters of European security but also those of European culture were being redefined, as the division of Europe ceased to exist and Europe—east and west—was finding new grounds for bonding in historical, cultural, and religious terms."[28]

---

[28]Gulnur Aybet, "Turkey and European Institutions," *The International Spectator*, Vol. XXXIV, No. 1 (January/March 1999), p. 107.

The EU's redefinition since 1989 has tended to highlight Turkey's distinctiveness. Many Europeans have never been entirely convinced that Turkey is really a part of Europe. During the Cold War these concerns about Turkey's "Europeanness" were largely subordinated to broader strategic considerations. But with the end of the Cold War and the effort to create a closer political and cultural union, these other social and cultural concerns have come more prominently to the fore. As Dutch Foreign Minister, Hans Van Mierlo, bluntly put it in early 1997: "There is a problem of a large Muslim state. Do we want that in Europe? It is an unspoken question."[29]

Turkey's troubled relations with Greece and its human rights record have also posed obstacles to its candidacy for EU membership. But Greece often provided a convenient excuse for other members to camouflage their own deep concerns about Turkey's eligibility for membership. As long as Greece vehemently opposed Turkish membership, they could hide behind Greece and let Greece take the brunt of Turkish anger and indignation.

The EU's failure to include Turkey on the list of potential candidates at the Luxembourg summit in December 1997 caused Ankara to freeze its relations with the EU and led to a sharp deterioration of Turkish-EU relations. However, since early 1999 relations have slowly improved. At its summit in Helsinki in December 1999, the EU officially invited Turkey to become a candidate member, thus fulfilling one of Ankara's most important foreign policy goals.

Two factors, in particular, contributed to the shift in the EU's position. The first was the change in government in Germany. The Kohl government had been one of the main opponents of Turkey's candidacy for EU membership. However, the SPD-Green coalition under Chancellor Gerhard Schröder adopted a more flexible and forward-leaning approach toward Turkey's candidacy.

The second important factor was a shift in the Greek position. In early September, Greece dropped its long-standing veto against EU financial assistance to Turkey and softened its objections to Turkey's

---

[29]Quoted in Stephen Kinzer, "Turkey Finds European Door Slow to Open," *New York Times,* February 23, 1997.

candidacy for membership.[30] The more flexible Greek position has been part of a broader shift in Greek policy toward Turkey (see below) and has helped to give the recent Greek-Turkish rapprochement greater impetus.

The EU's acceptance of Turkey's candidacy by no means eliminates all Turkey's problems with the EU. Negotiations on membership will not be opened until Turkey has met the Copenhagen criteria—including an improvement in its human rights performance—which could take quite a long time. However, the EU's decision removes an important political-psychological obstacle and puts Turkey's relations with the EU on a new, more positive footing. This could make some of the technical issues related to membership easier to resolve. The decision also weakens the hand of the Islamists, who have consistently argued that the rejection of Turkey's candidacy proved that Turkey's membership hopes were an illusion and that the country's salvation lay in closer ties to the Islamic world. Finally, the decision increases the prospects for reconciliation between Greece and Turkey. Greece's opposition to Turkey's EU candidacy was an important irritant in bilateral relations. With this obstacle removed, the chances for a broader improvement in Greek-Turkish relations are increased. An improvement in Greek-Turkish bilateral relations could also have a positive impact on the prospects for a Cyprus settlement over the long run.

NATO AND ESDI

At the same time, the European effort to create a distinct European Security and Defense Identity (ESDI) has raised new problems for Turkey. ESDI is problematic from Turkey's point of view because Turkey is not a member of the EU. Thus it is not involved in EU decisions that have a direct bearing on the security and defense dimensions of the EU's Common Foreign and Security Policy (CFSP) and the role of the West European Union (WEU). This problem could become more acute if the WEU is folded into the EU, as currently planned. If the functions of the WEU Council—in which Turkey

---

[30]Peter Norbert and Leyla Boulton, "Greece Supports EU and Package for Turkey," *Financial Times*, September 6, 1999. Also, "In a Shift, Greece Backs Turkey as EU Member," *International Herald Tribune*, September 6, 1999.

participates as an associate member—are taken over by the EU Council, Turkey fears it could find itself marginalized from any defense-related EU decisions.

These considerations have reinforced the importance of NATO in Turkish eyes. NATO provides the main multilateral vehicle for achieving Turkish security interests. Ankara thus opposes any weakening of NATO's role or effort to transfer greater planning and decisionmaking over defense matters to the EU. In addition, Turkey has insisted that non–EU allies must be involved in the planning and decisionmaking if the EU is going to draw on NATO assets in a crisis.

At the same time, NATO's own evolution could create new problems in Ankara's relations with the Alliance. Turkey is the only country in the Alliance that faces a serious threat to its borders (from Iraq and Syria). Ankara, thus, does not want to see a dilution of the Alliance's traditional emphasis on collective defense (Article V) and has been uncomfortable with the Alliance's emphasis on "new missions" and non–Article V contingencies.

Initially, Turkey also had reservations about NATO enlargement, fearing that it would antagonize Russia and possibly provoke Russia to strengthen its military presence in the Caucasus.[31] While in the end Turkey went along with the decision to expand the Alliance to Poland, Hungary, and the Czech Republic, Ankara would like to see a stronger focus on the Balkans in the future and is likely to push hard for the inclusion of Bulgaria and Romania in any second round of enlargement.

Turkey's growing engagement in the Middle East could also create problems for Turkey's relations with NATO. Many allies strongly oppose broadening of NATO's scope for action and want the Alliance to focus on security threats to the Euro-Atlantic area. Some allies might balk at aiding Turkey if it gets into a skirmish with one of its Middle Eastern neighbors, such as Iraq or Syria.[32] However, a failure of

---

[31]For a good discussion of Turkish concerns, see Ali L. Karaosmanoglu, "NATO Enlargement and the South," *Security Dialogue*, Vol. 30, No. 2 (June 1999), pp. 213–224.

[32]Germany's hesitant response to Turkey's request for Allied Mobile Force-Air reinforcements during the Gulf crisis highlights this problem. To many Germans, deterring a possible attack by Iraq against Turkey was not what NATO was all about. To many Turks, on the other hand, Germany's ambivalent response called into question

NATO to come to Turkey's aid in such a case could create a crisis in Turkey's relations with NATO and could even prompt Turkey to withdraw from the Alliance altogether.

GREECE AND CYPRUS

The Greek-Turkish dispute has been a major source of instability in the Eastern Mediterranean and a major concern for Greece and Turkey's NATO allies. In January 1996, the two countries nearly went to war over the islet of Imia/Kardak.[33] Only last-minute, high-level U.S. intervention prevented a possible military clash between the two countries. Moreover, in the wake of the incident, the air forces of both sides continued to engage in mock dogfights, increasing the risk that any inadvertent accident or incident could spiral out of control and lead to armed conflict.[34]

Recently, however, Greek-Turkish relations have begun to warm. In July 1999, the two countries opened a dialogue on nonsensitive issues such as trade, the environment, and tourism. This dialogue was given greater impetus by the earthquake in Turkey on August 19 and the one in September in Athens, which provoked an outburst of popular sympathy in both countries. This was followed by Greece's support for Turkey's EU candidacy at the Helsinki summit in December 1999 and a visit to Ankara by Greek Prime Minister George Papandreou in January 2000—the first visit by a Greek foreign minister to Turkey in nearly 40 years.

To date the dialogue has been limited to "low politics"—i.e., noncontroversial items such as trade and tourism. However, the success of these talks could lead to a broader dialogue on more sensitive is-

---

the validity of Article V (collective defense) of the Washington treaty and raised broader doubts about the utility of NATO membership. See Ian O. Lesser, *Bridge or Barrier: Turkey and the West After the Cold War*, Santa Monica, CA: RAND, R-4204-AF/A, 1992, pp. 14–15.

[33]Imia is the Greek name for the islet; Kardak is the Turkish name.

[34]In October 1997, Greece put its forces on alert after two Turkish planes violated Greek Cypriot airspace and tangled with two Greek fighter bombers. A few weeks later, Greek-Turkish warships collided during a Turkish naval exercise in the Aegean. In both cases, there were no serious injuries and a major confrontation was avoided, but the incidents underscored the danger of an inadvertent incident spiraling out of control and possibly leading to armed conflict between the two countries.

sues in the Aegean. Turkey has indicated that it would be willing to bring the continental shelf issue to the International Court of Justice in The Hague, a long-standing Greek demand. This is an important shift in Turkey's policy and could lay the basis for an eventual resolution of the continental shelf issue.

Cyprus remains a major irritant in relations. However, the EU's acceptance of Turkey's candidacy for EU membership, as well as the recent improvement in Greek-Turkish relations, add a new dynamic to the Cyprus equation and could eventually contribute to a settlement of the issue. Turkey now has a greater incentive for trying to achieve a settlement on Cyprus. A Cyprus settlement would not only give new impetus to the recent thaw in Greek-Turkish relations, but would also remove an important obstacle to Turkey's eventual membership in the EU.

However, a major breakthrough on the Cyprus issue seems unlikely in the near future. Within the Turkish Cypriot community, the parties that favor a more conciliatory approach to the Cyprus issue have lost support and are today weaker than they were several years ago. Nor is there any sign that Ankara is ready to put serious pressure on Rauf Denktash, the leader of the Turkish Cypriot community, to take a more conciliatory position. Denktash did agree to resume the UN-sponsored "proximity talks" in December 1999.[35] But there is little indication that he is about to drop his insistence that the Turkish Republic of Northern Cyprus (TRNC) be recognized as a coequal independent state—a nonstarter as far as the Greek Cypriots are concerned.

It is doubtful, moreover, whether either Turkey or the Turkish Cypriots would ever agree to the demilitarization of the island, as the Greek Cypriots have proposed. The Turkish military presence is seen by both Turkey and the Turkish Cypriots as a guarantee of the security of the Turkish Cypriot community. As noted earlier, Turkey increasingly sees this presence as integrally linked to its own security.[36]

---

[35]The proximity talks are designed to lay the groundwork for the resumption of intercommunal talks, which were broken off in August 1997.

[36]Prime Minister Ecevit underscored this point in his speech celebrating the 25th Anniversary of the Turkish intervention in July 1999: "As much as Turkey is the guar-

It compensates for Turkey's weakness vis-à-vis Greece in the Aegean. Hence, Ankara is likely to oppose any settlement that would lead to a significant reduction of this presence.

Several factors, however, could provide an incentive for progress over the medium term. A Greek-Turkish rapprochement that resolved the outstanding differences over the Aegean, for instance, could provide the much-needed impetus for the two countries to address the Cyprus problem. Moreover, if a real reconciliation with Greece were to occur, Turkey might feel less of a strategic imperative to retain a large military presence on Cyprus.

The EU's approach to Cyprus could also have an important influence on an eventual settlement. At the Helsinki summit in December 1999, the EU indicated that a Cyprus settlement would not be a precondition for the admission of the (Greek) Republic of Cyprus. Thus if a settlement of the Cyprus issue has not been achieved by the time of the completion of accession negotiations with the Greek Cypriot government, the EU might admit the Greek part of Cyprus. From the Turkish point of view, this would be highly disadvantageous, since Greek Cypriot membership would add another potential veto against Turkish accession to the EU. To avoid this, Turkey might be willing to make concessions that would facilitate a settlement.

THE AMERICAN CONNECTION

Close ties to the United States have always been important for Turkey. During the Cold War, the United States was seen as the main guarantor of Turkish security. While U.S.-Turkish relations have evolved substantially since then,[37] close ties to the United States remain an important cornerstone of Turkey's foreign policy.

However, the focus of the U.S.-Turkish relationship has shifted since the end of the Cold War. During the Cold War, the cornerstone of

---

antee of KKTC security, the KKTC is the guarantee of Turkish security." See "Turkey and KKTC Not Moving an Inch from Cyprus Policy," *Turkish Probe*, July 25, 1999.

[37] For a good discussion of these changes, see George S. Harris, *Troubled Alliance: Turkish-American Problems in Historical Perspective 1945–1971*, Washington, DC: AEI-Hoover Policy Studies, 1972. For a more recent discussion, see Lesser, *Bridge or Barrier: Turkey and the West After the Cold War*.

Turkish-American security was the need to deter a potential threat from the Soviet Union. Today, by contrast, Turkish-American security cooperation is focused primarily on the Middle East, the Caspian region, and the Balkans. This shift in focus has given Turkish-American relations an important new strategic dimension that did not exist during the Cold War.

At the same time, the deterioration of Turkey's ties with Europe has increased the importance of strong ties to the United States. The United States is seen by Turks as being more supportive of Turkey's security concerns than Europe. The United States has strongly backed Turkey's candidacy for EU membership and has lent strong political support to Ankara's effort to build the Baku-Ceyhan pipeline. Washington has also been more supportive of Turkey's struggle against the PKK than has Europe, which has generally been critical of Turkey's handling of the Kurdish issue.

This support has been greatly appreciated in Ankara and contributed to a deepening of Turkish-U.S. ties in recent years. Cooperation has been particularly intense in the Caspian Basin. Both countries share a common interest in promoting the independence and sovereignty of the states in the Caspian area, limiting Moscow's influence there, and developing the region's energy resources. As noted, the United States has strongly backed Turkey's plans for the construction of the Baku-Ceyhan pipeline and worked closely behind the scenes to get the Azerbaijan government and Western oil companies to support the Baku-Ceyhan project.

Ankara and Washington have also closely cooperated in the Balkans. Turkey played a key role in training the Muslim army in Bosnia under the U.S.-led "train and equip" program. Ankara also put several of its bases at the disposal of the United States and NATO during the Kosovo conflict. These moves have greatly contributed to strengthening the U.S.-Turkish security relationship and enhancing Turkey's strategic importance in U.S. eyes.

One of the important side benefits of this deepening bilateral cooperation is that relations with Turkey have been increasingly decoupled from Greek-Turkish relations. This has allowed the United States to pursue relations with Turkey on their own merits. At the same time, the United States has played an important behind-the-scenes role in encouraging the recent thaw in Greek-Turkish relations.

Turkish-U.S. relations, however, have been far from trouble free. Human rights and the Kurdish issue have become an increasing source of friction, especially with the U.S. Congress. In 1994, for instance, Turkey canceled the purchase of 10 Cobra helicopters—for which it had already paid—after Congress froze their delivery because of human rights concerns. More recently, the delivery of three frigates was postponed because of Congressional concern over Turkey's human rights record, though the Clinton Administration was eventually able to secure their release and delivery.

The increasing intrusion of human rights issues into the defense relationship has been a source of growing irritation in Ankara and has led Turkey to seek to diversify its defense procurement. One of the motivations for Ankara's efforts to deepen defense ties with Israel has been its desire to avoid the human rights–related hassles on defense purchases that it has faced of late in Europe and the United States. At the same time, the decision to phase out military assistance to Turkey (and Greece) has reduced Washington's ability to influence Turkish policy.

Important differences also exist between Ankara and Washington on key regional issues in the Middle East. Ankara is more inclined toward a policy of engagement with Iraq—especially economic engagement—than the United States, which has sought to isolate and contain Baghdad. Turkey also fears that Washington's efforts to topple Saddam Hussein could lead to the creation of a de facto Kurdish state on Turkey's border and thus exacerbate Turkey's internal struggle against Kurdish separatism. Hence, Turkey has imposed tight restrictions on the U.S. use of Incirlik and other Turkish air bases to monitor the no-fly zone over Northern Iraq.

Turkish and U.S. perspectives on Iran also differ considerably. Whereas the United States has generally sought to isolate Iran, Turkey prefers a policy of engagement. Ankara needs Iran's cooperation on the Kurdish issue. Iran is also a major source of energy supplies. The alternatives are Russia or Algeria, neither of which is a particularly attractive partner and both of which bring security problems that Ankara is eager to avoid. Thus, Turkey is unlikely to join U.S.-sponsored efforts to isolate Iran.

On Syria, U.S. and Turkish perspectives have been closer. Turkey viewed U.S. efforts to court Syria during the first Clinton Administration with suspicion because of Syria's support for the PKK. However, Turkish concerns have decreased since the expulsion of PKK leader Abdullah Öcalan in late 1998 and the subsequent thaw in Turkish-Syrian relations. Nevertheless, Ankara remains wary of any U.S.-backed peace initiative that might lead to a redeployment of Syrian troops along the Turkish-Syrian border or prejudice its discussions with Syria over water.

These differences make it unlikely that Turkey will allow the United States to use Turkish facilities in Middle East contingencies, except if Turkish national interests are directly threatened. In short, Özal's policy during the Gulf War is likely to be the exception, not the rule. Thus, it would be unwise for the United States to assume that Turkish bases will be available to the United States except in circumstances where Turkish territory or Turkish interests are directly threatened.

These differences also present important obstacles to the development of a broader "strategic partnership" between Washington and Ankara. At the same time, both sides have too much at stake to let relations seriously languish. For the United States, Turkey is at the nexus of three areas of increasing strategic importance for U.S. policy: the Caspian, the Middle East, and the Balkans. Thus, Washington has a strong strategic interest in maintaining close ties to Turkey. For Ankara, Washington remains an indispensable security partner, especially since its chances of becoming a member of the EU in the next decade are slim.

CONCLUSION: TURKEY'S STRATEGIC OPTIONS

Turkey's foreign and security policy is currently undergoing revision and redefinition in response to changes in Turkey's security environment as well as domestic pressures. Where this process will lead and exactly how it will affect Turkey's overall security orientation will depend on a number of factors, particularly U.S. and European policy. In principle, Turkey has several broad options:

- **European Option.** In this option, Turkey would strengthen its ties to Europe. EU membership would be a top Turkish priority and Turkey would accelerate efforts to achieve it. If the strategy were successful, this would complete the Atatürk revolution and end the ambivalence about Turkey's "Europeanness." There are, however, a number of problems with this option. First, European attitudes toward Turkish membership remain ambivalent. Thus Europe would have to adopt a more proactive approach to Turkish membership—something Europe has so far been reluctant to do. It would also require important changes in Turkey's own policy, especially toward Cyprus and the Kurdish issue—changes Turkey may not be willing to make. Third, it would take a long time. Even under the best of circumstances, Turkey would probably not be ready for membership for 15 to 20 years. The Turkish public might lose patience with the long delay, especially if it required heavy sacrifices and compelled Turkey to forgo other policy options considered to be in the Turkish national interest.

- **Eurasian Option.** In this option, Turkey would concentrate on strengthening ties to the newly independent states in Central Asia and the Caucasus. While not breaking ties to the West, Turkey would define itself more as a Eurasian power. This option has strong support in parts of the Turkish political spectrum, especially the Nationalist Action Party (MHP), which is a member of the current ruling coalition. This option, however, also has a number of weaknesses. First, it would heighten tensions with Russia, which has looked askance at Ankara's efforts to increase its influence in Central Asia and the Caucasus. It would also intensify rivalry with Iran, possibly driving Iran and Russia into a tacit alliance. Third, it could overstretch Turkish resources. All of the states in Central Asia and the Caucasus countries are poor and it will be quite a while before the impact of the energy bonus is felt—and even then the impact is likely to be considerably less than many observers initially expected.

- **Middle Eastern Option.** In this option, Turkey would emphasize its Islamic heritage and seek to strengthen ties to the Islamic countries of the Middle East and Asia. Here again, however, there are problems. For one thing, any effort to put an Islamic stamp on Turkish foreign policy would meet strong resistance from the Turkish military, who consider themselves the guardian of the Atatürk revolution and are the dominant influence on Turkish foreign policy. It would also be opposed by much of the Westernized elite, which dominates the bureaucracy, universities, and media. Finally, many Middle Eastern countries remain suspicious and mistrustful of Turkey because of its imperial past. Some also regard Turkey's emphasis on secularism as a betrayal of Islam. Hence they are likely to react with reserve to any attempt by Turkey to play a major role in the region.

- **Strategic Partnership with the United States.** In this option, Turkey would make a strategic partnership with the United States the centerpiece of its foreign policy. The problem is that this option was tried before (under Özal) and was never really successful. Moreover, it could run into domestic opposition from the Greek lobby in the U.S. Congress. Also, Turkish and U.S. approaches to a number of key issues in the Middle East— especially concerning Iran and Iraq—differ. Hence Turkey might be reluctant to embrace U.S. policies too closely for fear of damaging relations with either country.

- **Multidimensional Policy.** In this option, Turkey would pursue a multidimensional policy based more strongly on national interests. Ankara would still seek good relations with Europe, but EU membership would be less of an "obsession." Similarly, Turkey would maintain strong ties to the United States, but it would not seek to achieve a broad-based strategic partnership. At the same time, it would expand ties to some areas such as the Caucasus and Iraq even if these conflicted in some ways with Western policy.

In many ways, this is the most likely policy option. It would allow Turkey to preserve the essence of its traditional relationships but avoid the burdens of overdependence on any single one. It would also be in keeping with Turkey's traditional (i.e., pre–World War II) foreign policy, which avoided overtly siding with one particular country or group of countries. The downside is that this option might overstretch Turkey's resources and leave Turkey more isolated in the event of a crisis—always a danger given Turkey's location in a troubled and unstable neighborhood.

Regardless of which option—or combination of options—is eventually chosen, Turkey is likely to pursue a more assertive and active policy in the future, one which is less constrained than in the past. Such a policy would be in keeping with changes in Turkey's security environment since the end of the Cold War as well as with emerging trends in Turkey's domestic policies—above all, growing nationalism. Turkey will continue to maintain strong ties to the West, but be less disposed to automatically follow the U.S. lead when doing so conflicts with its narrow national interests. This will make managing relations with Ankara more difficult—and more challenging.

Chapter Four

WESTERN INTERESTS IN A CHANGING TURKEY

Ian O. Lesser

Along with changes on the domestic and regional levels, Turkey has been deeply affected by global changes in international relations over the last decade. The consequences for Ankara's policy toward specific regions and issues are examined elsewhere in this report. But it is useful to understand the ways in which broad-gauge changes on the geopolitical scene affect Turkey's role from a Western and, above all, an American perspective.[1] Western stakes in Turkey are substantial and continue to evolve in the post–Cold War era.

TRANSREGIONAL ISSUES AND OPPORTUNITIES

First, in a security environment increasingly characterized by "transregional" problems, Turkey is a transregional partner par excellence. Traditionally, U.S. national security strategy has made sharp distinctions between the security of key regions—European security, Middle Eastern security, Asian security, etc. As the defense of territory has become a less prominent concern in the wake of the Cold War, there has been a parallel rise in attention to transnational risks, from spillovers of terrorism and political violence, to the growing reach of ballistic missiles. In fact, these risks are not simply transnational, but, more significantly, transregional (i.e., cutting

---

[1]For a discussion from a European perspective, see Ludger Kühnhardt, "On Germany, Turkey and the United States," in Huseyin Bagci, Jackson Janes, and Ludger Kühnhardt (eds.), *Parameters of Partnership: The U.S.-Turkey-Europe*, Baden-Baden: Nomos Verlagsgesellschaft, 1999, pp. 217–235.

across regional security lines). Turkey has long viewed itself as a "bridge" in international relations, whereas the Western tendency, even after the Cold War, has been to see Turkey as a "barrier" to instability emanating from Eurasia and the Middle East.[2] The notion of Turkey as a borderland state, to use the terminology of early 20th-century geopoliticians, has considerable relevance in an era of transregional challenges. But today, Turkey is not simply a barrier to security risks, but also an increasingly capable and assertive actor in its own right, and potentially a more valuable partner in managing transregional problems; that is, problems that may have regional origins but are capable of influencing the security environment further afield. Such problems abound on Turkey's borders, from the Gulf and the Arab-Israeli dispute, to the Caucasus and the Balkans. New lines of communication for energy and nonenergy trade, converging in or near Turkey, reinforce this transregional role.[3]

CHANGING DEFINITION OF EUROPEAN SECURITY

A second related factor affecting Turkey's importance in U.S. perception concerns its role in relation to European security. European security has come to be defined in broader terms, as a result of the enlargement of NATO and its partners, and the growth of new Alliance missions, most of which are likely to be performed outside the traditional NATO area. In the new European environment, the most prominent risks are on Europe's southern periphery. Indeed, contingencies on Turkey's borders, or nearby, now represent the bulk of

---

[2]This theme is explored in Ian O. Lesser, "Bridge or Barrier? Turkey and the West After the Cold War," in Graham E. Fuller, Ian O. Lesser et al., *Turkey's New Geopolitics: From the Balkans to Western China*, Boulder, CO: Westview/RAND, 1993. The analysis is reassessed in Lesser, "Bridge or Barrier Revisited: Turkish Security Relations with the West," in Alan Makovsky and Sabri Sayari (eds.), *Changing Dynamics of Turkish Foreign Policy*, Washington, DC: Washington Institute for Near East Policy, forthcoming. A recent restatement of the "bridge" thesis can be found in Suleyman Demirel, "Turkey a Role Model at Turbulent Crossroads," *Special Policy Forum Report*, Washington, DC: Washington Institute for Near East Policy, April 30, 1999.

[3]Turkey's importance as part of the "strategic energy ellipse" is highlighted in Geoffrey Kemp and Robert E. Harkavy, *Strategic Geography and the Changing Middle East*, Washington, DC: Carnegie Endowment, 1997. See also Temel Iskit, "Turkey: A New Actor in the Field of Energy Politics?" *Perceptions* (Ankara), March–May 1996, pp. 58–82; and Bulent Gokay, "Caspian Uncertainties: Regional Rivalries and Pipelines," *Perceptions* (Ankara), March–May 1998, pp. 49–66.

the scenarios against which the Alliance must plan. Risks in Turkish relations with Iran, Iraq, and Syria are part of this equation, as is the potential for spillovers of refugees and instability in the Caucasus. Should Russia move to challenge U.S. and Western security interests in the future, it may choose to do so on the European periphery—in the eastern Mediterranean, the Balkans, the "near abroad," or the Middle East—rather than in Eastern Europe where recent geopolitical changes will be difficult to overturn. Turkey could therefore emerge as a leading partner in the longer-term security relationship with Russia. A history of Turkish-Russian strategic competition has produced a particularly wary attitude in Ankara, and Turkish strategists often worry about the prospect that Turkey may be left to deal with these residual Russian risks alone. Even as Ankara has enjoyed major successes in countering the Kurdistan Workers Party (PKK), the reconfiguration of the PKK's strategy and operations in the wake of the Öcalan trial introduce the possibility of more active Russian and Armenian support for Kurdish separatism, a development that would touch directly on Turkey's leading security concern.[4] The need for deterrence and reassurance with regard to Russia is likely to be a key motivator in Turkish relations with the United States. In the event of a deterioration of relations with Russia, Turkey could be of central importance to Washington for similar reasons. At the very least, Turkey will be highly exposed to the consequences of anarchy and chaos in the Black Sea and Caucasus regions—one reason that Turkish policymakers have been troubled by the crisis in Chechnya. This concern has also led Ankara to propose a stability pact for the south Caucasus that embraces Turkey, Georgia, and Azerbaijan.

Turkey may be a more important actor in an expanded European security space, but the institutional framework for this role is becoming less clear as the European Union (EU) develops a more ambitious foreign and security policy, potentially more independent from the United States and NATO.[5] Despite the apparent leap forward in Turkish-EU relations at Helsinki, the uncertain longer-term outlook

---

[4]This could also affect the political-risk climate for the Baku-Ceyhan pipeline. "Where, Oh Where, Has the PKK Gone?" *Stratfor.com*, August 30, 1999.

[5]For recent Turkish perspectives on NATO adaptation, see Suleyman Demirel, "Turkey and NATO at the Threshold of a New Century," and Gulnur Aybet, "NATO's New Missions," *Perceptions* (Ankara), March–May 1999, pp. 5–12.

for full Turkish membership in the EU makes Turkey a difficult fit. On the one hand, both the United States and Europe have a stake in engaging Turkey as an increasingly capable security partner adjacent to insecure regions. In the absence of a legitimate role in European security, Ankara's new foreign policy assertiveness, coupled with a more vigorous Turkish nationalism, may be a source of concern. On the other hand, Europe is not inclined to give Turkey, even as an EU "candidate," more than a peripheral say in its nascent foreign and security policy. Above all, Europe is wary of taking on new and potentially controversial security commitments on Turkey's behalf. If Europe is unable to develop an effective framework for integrating Turkey in its future foreign and security policy decisionmaking, Turkey's position in European security will become even more anomalous and more dependent on bilateral ties with the United States.[6] Turkey's EU candidacy coupled with a more serious commitment to building a common foreign and security policy in Brussels places these questions in sharper relief. It is now harder to leave Turkey outside Europe's defense decisionmaking, and Turkey can bring a good deal to the table. On the other hand, there is a greater European incentive to streamline decisionmaking, and greater sensitivity to the challenges imposed by having borders with Iran, Iraq, and Syria.

NEW SECURITY GEOMETRIES

Third, Turkey is at the center of a relatively recent phenomenon with important implications for U.S. strategy: the rise of new "security geometries," or new alliances in critical regions. The most prominent example has been the steadily expanding political, economic, and security relationship between Turkey and Israel. Jordan is a more ambivalent but potentially significant third partner in this equation.[7]

---

[6]This issue was the subject of intensive Turkish diplomacy at NATO's 1999 Washington Summit. The assurances offered to Turkey in the context of future WEU decisionmaking, while viewed as a success from Ankara, will likely prove insufficient over the longer term, as the WEU's own role is absorbed by the EU.

[7]These links have encouraged the rise of other new "geometries" involving Iran, Syria, Iraq, Armenia, and Greece. Russia and Serbia are also part of this equation. Despite reports of new security "agreements" involving some of these states, none appear comparable to the Israeli-Turkish relationship in substance or geopolitical significance.

Underlying these new relationships is the dominant role of the United States as an international partner for all three countries. The United States stands to gain considerably from these alignments of allied states, as a contribution to power balances in the Middle East, and as an alternative set of partners in the management of regional problems and in power projection for the Gulf. In a less direct fashion, the growth of Turkish ties with the Turkic republics of the Caucasus and Central Asia, although more modest than envisioned in the early 1990s, makes Turkey an important counterweight to Russian, Iranian, and Chinese influence. Ankara's much improved relations in the Balkans, including new bilateral ties with Bulgaria, the Former Yugoslav Republic of Macedonia (FYROM), and Albania, also make Turkey a more important player in this sphere.

A PIVOTAL STATE?

The end of the Cold War and the emergence of a more fluid international environment have encouraged a revival of geopolitical thinking and the rediscovery of neglected regions (e.g., Central Asia). Absent Cold War imperatives, the American foreign policy debate has focused, increasingly, on the question of interests (broadly or narrowly construed) and modes of action (multilateral or unilateral). A full discussion of these tendencies in the current debate is beyond the scope of this analysis. But different worldviews and foreign policy preferences imply different conceptions of Turkey's strategic importance and different views of Ankara as an ally.

Only the narrowest ("homeland defense") approach to U.S. interests places Turkey outside the definition of an important ally. As a contributor to European, Middle Eastern, and Eurasian futures, Turkey is arguably unique. An emphasis on the transregional challenges noted above underscores this point. The phrase "location, location, location" has considerable relevance in the Turkish case.[8] But this geographic approach is only a starting point, albeit an important one, especially in relation to the projection of military power, lines of communication for resources, and trade. Location implies a potential for regional influence; it does not ensure it (as the relatively lim-

---

[8]See Alan Makovsky, "Marching in Step, Mostly!" *Private View* (Istanbul), Spring 1999, pp. 30–38.

ited nature of Turkey's external policy from the formation of the Republic through the 1980s demonstrates). In the absence of agreement on the Turkish side, it also does not ensure that Turkey's allies will be able to derive any advantage from Turkey's valuable position.

Ankara is, unusually, an attractive international partner for multilateralists and unilateralists alike. For the former, Turkey's NATO role, growing potential for regional action (diplomatic, economic, and military), and coalition approach to critical regions such as the Balkans is attractive. For the latter, selective cooperation with capable partners remains useful, and Turkey's ability to facilitate U.S. power projection and preference for close bilateral ties count heavily. Skeptics with regard to European defense initiatives tend to see Turkey as one of the few "serious" security partners for contingencies outside the center of Europe. Moreover, U.S. interests in adjacent regions are hardly transient, and are among the most durable in U.S. foreign policy. Turkish strategists periodically worry about the potential for declining interest in Turkey as a result of the resolution of regional problems. It requires extraordinary optimism to imagine the confluence of a smooth transition to a reformed, benign Russia; the absence of instability in the Caucasus, Central Asia, and the Balkans; the full resolution of Arab-Israeli disputes; the disappearance of interstate frictions in the Gulf; and the end of Greek-Turkish conflict. Some of these transitions are attainable (and, in the case of Greek-Turkish relations, are arguably under way). But the multiple sources of instability on Turkey's borders argue for a continuing U.S. stake. Moreover, the U.S. stake in Turkey is a product of opportunities as well as challenges. These may expand to the extent that longstanding regional problems are resolved (e.g., the potential for Turkey to play a key role in regional development and reconstruction in the Balkans or the Middle East).

Turkey's human rights problems are more problematic in the context of an American foreign policy that has in recent years come to rely heavily on notions of "democratic enlargement," the promotion of international norms, and doctrine of humanitarian intervention.[9] The normalization of Turkey with regard to human rights issues and,

---

[9]See the discussion in Joseph S. Nye, Jr., "Redefining the National Interest," *Foreign Affairs*, July/August 1999, pp. 22–35.

above all, the resolution of the Kurdish problem, would likely have a transforming effect on the character of bilateral relations.[10] It would also have a potentially transforming effect on the prospect for Turkish integration in Europe, and therefore on the future balance in Ankara's relations with the West as a whole. There is considerable irony in the fact that U.S. policy looks to Turkey as a partner in reform and stability in several key regions, yet finds Turkey's own difficulties in these areas the leading obstacle to closer cooperation. This tension is arguably most pronounced for American multilateralists given their natural emphasis on norms in internal and external behavior. This dilemma is not unique to Turkey, and occurs elsewhere in U.S. foreign policy, notably in relation to China, where the balance between cooperation and alienation is also critical.[11]

Turkey has been evocatively described as a "pivot" state.[12] Population, location, and economic potential (one might add military power and potential) are key requirements for pivot status. But the defining quality of a pivotal state is, above all, the capacity to affect regional and international stability. By this measure, Turkey clearly qualifies, along with such states as Mexico, Brazil, Algeria, Egypt, India, and Indonesia. This disparate list is bound together by the fact that developments in these states hold the capacity for transregional progress—or mayhem. [13]

> At a multifold crossroads between East and West, North and South, Christendom and Islam, Turkey has the potential to influence countries thousands of miles from the Bosporus. . . . Turkey enjoys solid economic growth and middle class prosperity. However, it also shows many of the difficulties that worry other pivotal states: popu-

---

[10]For the most recent official U.S. assessment of the human rights situation in Turkey, see U.S. Department of State, *Turkey Country Report on Human Rights Practices for 1998*, Washington, DC: Bureau of Democracy, Human Rights and Labor, U.S. Department of State, February 1999.

[11]This aspect of contemporary U.S. policy has had sharp critics. See, for example, Michael Mandelbaum, "Foreign Policy as Social Work," *Foreign Affairs*, January/February 1996, pp. 16–32.

[12]Robert S. Chace, Emily Hill, and Paul Kennedy, "Pivotal States and U.S. Strategy," *Foreign Affairs*, Volume 75, No. 1, January/February 1996, pp. 33–51. See also Alan Makovsky's chapter in the volume based on this article, Robert Chace et al. (eds.), *The Pivotal States*, New York: Norton, 1999.

[13]Chace et al., p. 37.

lation and environmental pressures, severe ethnic minority challenges. . . . A prosperous, democratic, tolerant Turkey is a beacon
for the entire region; a Turkey engulfed by civil wars and racial and
religious hatreds, or nursing ambitions to interfere abroad, would
hurt American interests in innumerable ways and concern everyone
from pro-NATO strategists to friends of Israel.[14]

The "pivot" analysis takes as its starting point the traditional image of
Turkey as a geopolitical bridge, and goes on to argue that short of
preventing great power conflicts, applying energy and resources to
ensure the success of pivotal states such as Turkey should be the
most important goal of post–Cold War U.S. foreign policy. What
sets Turkey apart from the developing countries commonly viewed
as regional pivots is its membership in the Western strategic "club,"
principally through NATO, but also through a deepening relationship
with the EU.[15] Thus developments in Turkey are even more directly
linked to U.S. and Western interests. Consider, for example, the effect on the future of the Alliance, including the enlargement process,
of Turkish conflict with Greece—or Russia. By this measure, Turkey
is a pivot state par excellence.

Turkey's sheer scale is also a factor in geopolitical calculations.
Turkey's population in 1999 is roughly 65 million. Even with a population growth rate that is now only 1.4 percent, Turkey will shortly
have a larger population than Germany, the largest member of the
EU, although continued declines in the population growth rate suggest that Turkey's population by the middle of the 21st century may
still fall short of the 100 million mark.[16] These figures add a dimension of scale to political and economic arguments about Turkey
within the EU and regionally. Issues of integration, competition, and
cooperation with Turkey become compelling in Brussels or Athens,

---

[14]Chace et al., pp. 47–48.

[15]This makes Turkey unique in terms of other recent arguments about where U.S.
"intrinsic" and "extrinsic" interests are engaged. See Michael C. Desch, "The Keys
That Lock Up the World: Identifying American Interests in the Periphery," *International Security*, Vol. 14, No. 4 (Summer 1989), pp. 86–121. Turkey is arguably of both
intrinsic and extrinsic interest to the United States.

[16]*Turkey's Window of Opportunity; Demographic Transition Process and Its Consequences* (Istanbul: TUSIAD, 1999), p. 18. Onur Oymen's recently published
Turkiye'nin Gucu (Turkey's Strength) discusses demographic factors as a component
of Turkish power and potential.

in part, because of the sheer size of the country. In a related measure, it is notable that Turkey has the second largest military establishment in NATO, exceeded only by the United States.

THINKING THROUGH U.S. STAKES

Changes in the internal and external environment have made Turkey more, not less pivotal in strategic terms. But what precisely are the U.S. stakes in Turkey toward the 21st century? The following discussion identifies three broad concepts of U.S. concern: first, Turkey as a stable, democratic ally; second, Turkey as a positive actor in regional security and development; and third, Turkey as a contributor to U.S. freedom of action.

Stability and Democracy

Turkey's domestic evolution is of particular interest for the United States in the sense that democratization, prosperity, and stability in Turkey will continue to set the parameters for bilateral relations in the future. Leaving aside Greek-Turkish relations and the Cyprus issue, Turkey's internal situation has, historically, been a leading source of constraint on the bilateral relationship and Turkish-Western relations more generally. Indeed, the Western preoccupation with developments inside Turkey has a long history, dating back to the Ottoman Empire and its perceived decadence and resistance to reform. Republican Turkey too has often been analyzed "from the inside out" by Western observers. The current debate about the implications of social and political change within Turkey is only the most recent manifestation of a tendency to view Turkey's international role as determined by domestic developments. The internal focus has, if anything, been reinforced over the last decade by the disappearance of overwhelming Cold War imperatives, the emergence of "democratic enlargement" as a feature of NATO, and EU as well as U.S. policy. Turkey's own inclinations have also played a role, with internal issues dominating Turkish national security thinking in a way that is unique within NATO.

The confluence of these factors has resulted in close U.S. scrutiny of the domestic Turkish scene, with extraordinary focus on human rights and the continuing process of democratization. Attention has been further encouraged by the increasingly active debate on these issues within Turkey itself.[17] The human rights situation has been especially problematic and probably represents the leading obstacle to a closer and more effective strategic relationship. It directly affects the ability of the United States to deliver on arms transfers, themselves an important measure of the health of the bilateral relationship as seen from Ankara. If, for example, Congress does not approve pending coproduction agreements for attack helicopters or main battle tanks, in part because of human rights concerns, Turkish-U.S. relations will be dealt a severe blow. Human rights concerns have also shaped the environment on other issues of importance to the bilateral relationship, from support for Caspian oil pipelines to trade and investment. U.S. policy in the 1990s has consistently urged Ankara to "take risks for democracy" both because there is a strong tradition of this in U.S. foreign policy, and out of a realization that lack of reform spells a troubled relationship at many levels. U.S. reports on the human rights situation in Turkey remain sharply critical.[18] Indeed, if Turkey were to apply for NATO membership today, it is arguable that its application would be rejected on the basis of human rights problems, concerns about civilian control of the military, and the persistence of conflicts on its borders—criteria that have been rigorously applied in the NATO enlargement process.[19] Even from a narrower strategic perspective, it is clear that the full potential for regional security cooperation with Turkey (e.g., in the Balkans, the Middle East, and elsewhere) will be difficult to capture if human rights concerns are not effectively addressed.

Indirectly, U.S. interests are also affected by the even more serious consequences human rights matters have had for relations between Ankara and the EU. European analysts and policymakers have

---

[17]For a collection of mainstream Turkish perspectives, see *Perceptions* (Ankara), Vol. III, No. 4 (December 1998–February 1999), "Special Issue on Human Rights."

[18]See U.S. Department of State, *Turkey Country Report on Human Rights Practices for 1998.*

[19]The issue of civil-military relations is also sensitive on the Turkish side. The Turkish military, for its own reasons, does not wish to encourage the view that they are valid interlocutors on domestic as well as security issues. This has been cited as one reason for a recent Turkish General Staff (TGS) refusal to receive a visiting U.S. congressional delegation. See remarks by then Turkish Minister of Defense Hikmet Sami Turk on "Turkish Defense Policy," WINEP, Washington, March 3, 1999.

tended to take a harder line with Ankara on issues of human rights and political reform, with Turkey's domestic difficulties tending to reinforce the perception that Turkey is an important Middle Eastern rather than European partner. The circumscribed nature of the EU's relations with Turkey have, in turn, complicated U.S. policy by placing additional pressure on the bilateral relationship with Washington. The domestic situation also makes it more difficult for the United States to argue convincingly for Turkish integration in European institutions. All of these factors will continue to play a role in the European evaluation of Turkey's candidacy in light of the "Copenhagen criteria." This is a long-term prospect in which increasing EU scrutiny will be balanced against the likelihood of continued, positive change in Turkish society and politics.

Political reform, including progress on human rights, may also have a pronounced effect on Turkish external policy. A stable political scene, including the reinvigoration of the centrist political class, would likely allow a more predictable and less overtly nationalist foreign policy. A Turkey that is "doing well," with a self-confident leadership, might also be inclined to take the political risks necessary for sustained détente with Greece, and perhaps, new approaches to the conflict in the southeast. (It is noteworthy that Atatürk and Özal, at the height of their political careers, were able to engineer improvements in relations with Athens.) In the post-Helsinki climate there are signs that this is happening, with salutary effects in the Aegean and elsewhere. Economic reform, including more ambitious privatization policies, would likely create a more favorable climate for U.S. investment and assist Turkey to fulfill its promise as a "big emerging market."[20] In short, the Turkey that "matters most" to the United States is one that has undertaken the economic and political reforms necessary for Turkey to feel confident about its identity and its future in the West.[21]

By contrast, turmoil in politics and the economy would drain the energies of the key actors in Turkish foreign and security policy, from

---

[20]It is noteworthy that Turkey had a negative growth rate in 1999 for the first time in several years; this is a reflection of the economic impact of the devastating 1999 earthquake.

[21]Richard Perle, "A Turkish Story: The First Annual Robert Strausz-Hupe Lecture," *Foreign Policy Research Institute Wire*, Vol. 7, No. 11 (September 1999).

the military to the private sector, and inhibit a more active and positive role in regional affairs. The inability of successive Turkish governments to develop a coherent scheme of incentives for construction of the Baku-Ceyhan pipeline offers an example. Overall, the success of the Turkish economy, perennially on the verge of "takeoff," will have a considerable influence on the ability of Washington and Ankara to move toward a more diverse, "enhanced" strategic relationship in which security cooperation is augmented by better trade and investment ties, and regional joint ventures outside the military sphere.

The United States also has an interest in promoting positive change within Turkey so that Turkey can serve as a model for development elsewhere. The notion of Turkey as a model has been a recurrent fashion in Washington and Ankara since the end of the Cold War, especially in relation to the Caucasus and Central Asia. Movement in the Middle East peace process and regime changes in the Middle East have brought similar issues of reform and democratization to the fore. Policymakers in the United States and Turkey will undoubtedly wish to make the case for Turkey as a regional model in this setting (and in the Balkans). Resistance to this idea is more likely to emanate from Turkey's neighbors—who might well want Turkey as an economic and perhaps a security partner, but who dislike the notion of Turkey as a "model" for cultural and historical reasons.[22] More broadly, it is unclear whether the notion of regional models will retain its relevance in an era of globalization where trends are set by preferences and policies emanating from New York or Tokyo—or perhaps no longer "set" by states at all.[23]

---

[22]Arab ambivalence toward Turkey as a model is especially pronounced as a result of the Ottoman experience, modern Turkish secularism, and Ankara's NATO ties. See Philip Robins, *Turkey and the Middle East,* London: Royal Institute of International Affairs, 1991; Amikam Nachmani, *Turkey and the Middle East,* Ramat Gan: BESA, 1999; and Sabri Sayari "Turkey and the Middle East in the 1990s," *Journal of Palestine Studies*, Vol. xxxvi/3, No. 103, 1997.

[23]For a discussion of Turkish planning objectives in an era of globalization, see Orhan Guvenen, "Turkey's Medium and Long-Term Strategic Objectives: TR2007/15-TR 2017/9," *Perceptions* (Ankara), December–February 1999, pp. 5–20.

A Positive Regional Actor

As Turkey emerges as a more capable and active power, Washington will have a strong stake in encouraging Ankara to play a positive role in regional security and development.[24] At the level of general regional aims, American and Turkish interests are broadly congruent. Ankara and Washington speak in similar terms about the need for peace, stability, and economic development in the Balkans, the Middle East, and Eurasia. When examined in greater detail, there is considerable divergence in policy approaches to some key regions. In general, Turkish policy toward the Balkans has been almost entirely congruent with U.S. interests and preferences. As noted earlier, Ankara has pursued an active but very positive policy, normalizing relations with key neighbors such as Bulgaria, and adopting a multilateral approach to regional security (e.g., through participation in IFOR, SFOR, and KFOR; by leading the formation of a multinational peacekeeping force for the Balkans; and by authorizing the use of airbases in Thrace during the latter stages of Operation Allied Force).[25] Turkish F-16s flew missions from Italy during the Kosovo crisis, and Ankara was among the most active contributors to NATO humanitarian relief activities.

With regard to Russia and the former Soviet Union, Ankara has, similarly, played a positive role from a U.S. perspective. Close Turkish-Russian economic ties, restraint in policy toward the Caucasus (especially Chechnya and Azerbaijan) where Turkish interests and affinities are engaged, and a role in diversifying the political and economic ties of the newly independent states (e.g., Baku-Ceyhan as part of a "multiple-route" arrangement for Caspian oil exports) are all part of this equation.[26] In the event of a sharp deterioration in strategic relations with Moscow and a resurgent military threat,

---

[24]See Antony Blinken, "The Future of U.S.-Turkish Relations," Turgut Ozal Memorial Lecture, Washington Institute for Near East Policy, December 8, 1999.

[25]Ankara and Athens were leading forces behind the formation in 1998 of the Southeast European Brigade (SEEBRIG) involving seven Balkan states.

[26]Arguably, it is the diversification of energy routes rather than simply "an oil route for Turkey" that has driven U.S. policy in support of Baku-Ceyhan. Other routes, including proposed trans-Balkan lines, have also attracted favorable U.S. attention. See "Trans-Balkan Pipeline Complicates U.S.-Turkey Relations," *Stratfor.com*, January 14, 2000.

Ankara would once again play a critical containment role. Friction, to the extent that it exists in this setting, comes from Turkish concern over U.S. policy toward the East. In sharp contrast to burgeoning economic relations, Turkish observers tend to take a more pessimistic view of Russian futures and the potential for a renewed Russian military threat to Western interests. Unlike the situation in the Gulf, for example, the view from Ankara is more likely to be that U.S. policy toward Moscow is too soft, rather than too tough. There is a widespread perception in Turkey that Washington, while supportive, has not thrown its full weight behind the Baku-Ceyhan pipeline for fear of provoking a strongly negative reaction in Moscow. The reality, made evident at the Organization for Security and Cooperation in Europe (OSCE) summit in Istanbul in November 1999, is that the United States fully endorses Baku-Ceyhan, but looks to the private sector to finance this costly project.

Since the Gulf War, U.S. interests in Turkey as a partner in the Middle East have come to the fore. Here, the record and the outlook are mixed. Turkey's increasingly close and diverse relationship with Israel is an especially positive development from the U.S. perspective, bringing together separate strands of U.S. policy, enhancing the security of two key allies, and opening new avenues for trilateral and even wider regional cooperation. The Turkish-Israeli relationship places useful pressure on Syria, Iraq, and Iran and could enhance Washington's ability to address specific issues such as theater ballistic missile defense and terrorism. In the event of a comprehensive Arab-Israeli settlement, Turkey could also have much to offer as a partner in economic development, infrastructure projects, and as a source of "water for peace." Ankara's interest in the latter is, however, mixed. As a water surplus state, Turkey's regional influence could be enhanced by new water-supply arrangements. On the other hand, Ankara is concerned that its resources are not taken for granted, or its interests put on the table in the rush to achieve new peace agreements.

In the Gulf, where U.S. interests are heavily engaged, the outlook is less clear. Turkey has been an important base for power projection for the Gulf over the last decade (as during the Cold War). Incirlik, Batman, Mus, and other bases were heavily used during the Gulf War, and Turkish forces themselves made an important contribution by tying down Iraqi forces in the north. Above all, the closure of

Turkish oil pipelines and Turkish participation in the sanctions against Iraq have been a key component in the economic isolation of Baghdad—at massive economic cost to Ankara (Iraq had been Turkey's leading trade partner prior to the Gulf War). Operations Provide Comfort and Northern Watch have been instrumental to the policy of containment and the enforcement of the no-fly zone in northern Iraq, and have turned on access to Incirlik airbase.

But Ankara's own policy preferences on Iraq and Iran differ from those of Washington in important respects. With regard to Iraq, Turkey would clearly prefer to see an end to the costly sanctions regime (despite its own concerns about Iraqi weapons-of-mass-destruction [WMD] programs), and would probably accept a reassertion of full Iraqi sovereignty in the north as a means of controlling any residual PKK operations across the border. Although Ankara tolerates the ongoing air campaign against targets in the northern no-fly zone, Turkey has adopted an arm's-length attitude toward wider military operations (as in Operation Desert Fox) against Baghdad. Overall, Ankara regards Iraq as a difficult neighbor with whom it must ultimately coexist. The notion of an open-ended containment strategy does not fit well in this framework. Turkish strategists are also skeptical about multilateral approaches to Gulf security in the face of an overwhelmingly important American role.[27]

Turkey has a similarly important place in U.S. strategy toward Iran, where, for the moment, it would suit U.S. interests to have Ankara as an active participant in the policy of containment. Turkey has its own sources of friction with Iran, including concerns about Iranian support for Turkish Islamists and the PKK.[28] But, even more clearly than in the case of Iraq, political and economic engagement with Iran is a policy preference for Turkey. Turkey's interest in access to Iranian energy is an important factor in this regard (the United States, by contrast, objects to Turkish gas imports from Iran, and sees Turkey itself as an alternative to reliance on a more convenient Iranian route for the export of Caspian oil). The Turkish approach to

---

[27]See, for example, Aylin Seker, "The Fallacy of Multilateralism: The UN Involvement in the Gulf War and Its Aftermath," *Perceptions* (Ankara), June–August 1999, pp. 196–213.

[28]The recent revelations regarding Turkish Hizbullah have revived periodic Turkish accusations of Iranian assistance to Islamists in Turkey.

both Iran and Iraq is, in general, closer to the mainstream European view than to that of the United States. This approach may well be strengthened to the extent that Turkey leans toward EU foreign and security policy initiatives.

Turkish and U.S. approaches to Syria are broadly congruent although, as with Russia, Ankara is more wary and has historically pressed for a harder line on Syrian support for terrorism (i.e., the PKK) and other issues. As with the water issue, there is some concern that Washington—and Israel—include suitable arrangements to forestall the redeployment of Syrian forces to the north in the event of a Syrian-Israeli disengagement. Relations with Syria have been a leading outlet for the new activism in Turkish policy toward the Middle East at the end of the 1990s. To a point, this assertiveness has been convergent with U.S. policy interests, but the need to keep Damascus engaged in the peace process and concerns about reactions in Europe impose certain limits. The United States, and NATO, would certainly be obliged to assist Turkey in the event of any conflict with Syria. But a NATO consensus could be difficult to achieve, especially if the Kurdish insurgency provides the flashpoint. From a U.S. perspective, therefore, Turkish policy toward Syria is delicately poised between positive and negative influences.

Finally, Washington looks to Turkey to play a positive role in the Aegean and the eastern Mediterranean. Here, the experience has traditionally been most difficult, although the new thaw in Greek-Turkish relations starting in 1999 suggests that the environment is changing rapidly and positively.

The dynamics of the Greek-Turkish dispute are addressed elsewhere in this report. But from the perspective of U.S. interests, resolution— or at least a reduction of risk—in Greek-Turkish relations is a key objective. The Cyprus dispute, in particular, remains an obstacle to Congressional support for a more expansive relationship with Turkey. At the same time, the scope for a more flexible Turkish approach to Cyprus and the Aegean has appeared to narrow in recent years with the growth of nationalist sentiment within Turkey and the possibility that the "Turkish Republic of Northern Cyprus" (TRNC) and Ankara could respond to EU-Cyprus membership negotiations by a de facto merger of the Turkish side with Turkey proper. Such a development would effectively end the potential for a settlement on the island and make this source of tension in relations with the United States a permanently operating factor. The post-Helsinki atmosphere in Turkish-EU and Turkish-Greek relations makes this damaging possibility more remote.

There may be little strategic rationale for conflict between Greece and Turkey, but the risk of an accidental clash, and the potential for escalation touches directly on U.S. interests. The United States has an obvious stake in preventing conflict between two close allies. More significantly, the United States has a stake in preventing conflict that could negatively affect the geostrategic equation in Europe and the Middle East. Possible broader consequences of a clash over Cyprus or the Aegean include the open-ended estrangement of Turkey from Western institutions, making Ankara a far more difficult partner for Washington to engage in any form (this could include the loss of access to Incirlik airbase); casting of a shadow over future NATO enlargement and adaptation; and the deepening of "civilizational" cleavages in the Balkans and around the Mediterranean. Russia, Syria, and Iran could also become involved in ways that would work against U.S. security interests in the eastern Mediterranean, the Middle East, and the Caucasus. Even continued brinkmanship in the region, short of actual conflict, complicates the outlook for improved U.S.-Turkish relations across the board. Thus, second only to promoting the stable, internal evolution of Turkey, Washington has a key "enabling" stake in risk reduction and strategic dialogue between Greece and Turkey.[29]

With the potential for continued rapprochement between Ankara and Athens, the U.S. and the West as a whole have a strong stake in seeing tentative steps toward better relations deepened and extended. Washington, the EU, and NATO can contribute in different ways to this process. Washington and NATO can facilitate the implementation of military confidence-building measures in the Aegean, and provide opportunities for joint Greek-Turkish initiatives

---

[29]It is noteworthy that the 1999 earthquake has had a salutary effect on Greek-Turkish relations, with Greece providing some highly symbolic emergency assistance. This assistance was very well received in Turkey (with some notable exceptions in nationalist circles), and follows a steady improvement in the diplomatic climate in the months preceding the disaster. It has formed the basis for more positive steps in the wake of these disasters.

in the Balkans and the eastern Mediterranean. With the approval of Turkey's candidate status, and the decision to move ahead with accession negotiations for Cyprus, Brussels now has far greater leverage and credibility with all sides, although much will depend on the longer-term nature of Europe's engagement with Turkey. If Helsinki proves to have given Turkey a "hollow" candidacy, the inevitable disillusionment in Ankara could spill over into relations with Greece and will return Washington to center stage in this equation. To the extent that Greek-Turkish relations continue to evolve positively, this should remove a leading constraint on strategic cooperation between Washington and Ankara.

The current environment encourages U.S. interest in Turkey that is more balanced, in regional terms, than has generally been the case in the past. In the period since 1945, Turkey's importance in American eyes has been defined alternately in Middle Eastern and European terms, driven by the security concerns of the moment. Thus, in the early years of the Cold War, Turkey was seen as a key contributor to security in the "Northern Tier" comprising Greece, Turkey, Iran, and Afghanistan, and a barrier to Soviet aggression in the Middle East.[30] Over time, Ankara came to be seen as a part of the larger European security equation, not least because Ankara itself encouraged this Westward-looking focus. Successive crises in the Middle East, culminating in the Gulf War, cast Turkey once again in a Middle Eastern role. Today, with pressing security challenges from the Balkans to the Middle East and Eurasia, Turkey's strategic relevance is more diverse and, as noted earlier, essentially transregional. With the steady expansion of Turkey's own foreign policy horizons, Turkish policy elites are now more comfortable with a role that looks south and east, as well as toward Europe. But this new diversity in Turkish interests also means many more points of potential friction with key partners—above all, the United States.

---

[30]The evolution of Western policy in this context is treated in detail in Bruce Kuniholm, *The Origins of the Cold War in the Near East: Great Power Conflict and Diplomacy in Iran, Turkey and Greece* (Princeton: Princeton University Press, 1980).

Enhancing U.S. Freedom of Action

Beyond Turkey's potential to play a positive role in regions of importance to U.S. strategy, the United States has an interest in Turkey as a direct contributor to U.S. freedom of action—in essence, power projection—in adjacent regions. This aspect of the bilateral relationship came to the fore during the Gulf War, and has remained an important and controversial aspect of relations. Recognition of the importance of Turkey as a base for projecting military power was also a feature of Cold War planning, in which Turkey was not only a glacis confronting Soviet military power in Thrace and the Caucasus, but also a base for intelligence gathering and, in the event of conflict, the conduct of strategic attacks on targets within the Soviet Union.

Despite concerns in Ankara that the end of the Cold War would reduce Turkey's strategic importance to Washington, Turkey has become even more central to planning for the projection of military power. The fact that the Özal government permitted the United States to use Incirlik airbase and other facilities for offensive air operations against Iraq during the Gulf War encouraged the belief that Ankara would welcome a more forward-leaning approach to access and overflight. In reality, the Turkish contribution to coalition operations was highly controversial within the Turkish security establishment. The TGS in particular was wary of hyperactive participation in the air war (the chief of staff resigned during the Gulf crisis, reportedly over this question). Sovereignty concerns were central to this debate, and remained divisive throughout the period of Operation Provide Comfort. On occasions since the Gulf War when renewed U.S. air strikes on WMD and other targets in Iraq have been threatened or carried out, Turkish facilities have not been used. During the Iraqi incursion into the north in October 1996, and again during Operation Desert Fox, Ankara made it clear that the use of Turkish bases would not be welcome. This reticence can be ascribed to a closer measurement of Turkish interests in defense cooperation, and concern that a more provocative stance toward Baghdad might complicate Turkey's campaign against the PKK. Turkish policymakers, including the military, worry that they will be left to address the consequences of a wider confrontation with Iraq on Turkey's borders, while U.S. military intervention is aimed at containment rather than a definitive change in the regional order. In the event of a full-scale Western military campaign aimed at regime change in Baghdad, the Turkish response might well be favorable—as it was during the Gulf War. Today, against a background of rising nationalism, the Turkish interest in having a "seat at the table" in the context of large-scale security initiatives is arguably even greater than in the early 1990s.

That said, the extent of the air operations in the northern no-fly zone being conducted by U.S. and British aircraft flying from Incirlik reveals that Turkish policymakers, especially the TGS, are willing to tolerate such operations when convenient and compatible with Turkish security interests.[31] Recent Turkish successes in countering the PKK have put Ankara in a more confident mood vis-à-vis the situation in northern Iraq. Operation Northern Watch may also have some utility (e.g., intelligence sharing, control of the airspace, and reassurance against Iraqi retaliation) as an adjunct to Turkey's own cross-border operations against the PKK within what has become a de facto security zone across the border.

Looking ahead, the United States and Western allies may have even greater interest in Turkey as a base for air operations and the logistical support of ground operations in adjacent regions. As U.S. planners become increasingly concerned about reliance on bases and defense relationships within the Gulf for the defense of the political order and the region's resources, other power projection options may become more attractive. Bases such as Incirlik in southern Turkey are actually closer to the northern Gulf than facilities on the Arabian Peninsula. Concerns about political acceptance, regime stability, and terrorism in relation to deployed forces will be less pressing in Turkey than in the Gulf states. A northern route for power projection in the Gulf, relying on Turkey and perhaps Israel and Jordan, may also be more suitable to U.S. strategy, which is increasingly expeditionary in character.

U.S. and NATO interest has tended to focus on Incirlik for power projection purposes, but Turkey has a variety of bases that might be

---

[31]Some discomfort with the Operation Northern Watch mission persists. Former Defense Minister Hikmet Sami Turk, for example, has suggested while in office that the no-fly zone creates an "authority vacuum" in northern Iraq that is exploited by PKK terrorists. March 3, 1999, speech at the Washington Institute for Near East Policy, summarized in *PolicyWatch* #374 (Washington: WINEP), March 15, 1999.

useful for contingencies in the Balkans, the Caucasus, or the Caspian. The offer of facilities in Turkish Thrace during Operation Allied Force points to these alternatives, and suggests that Ankara is capable of prompt decisionmaking about the use of these facilities in a crisis.[32] Nonetheless, it is likely that the NATO context for Operation Allied Force was critical in Turkish perception. A unilateral request from the U.S. might not have been viewed favorably. Indeed, Ankara has always made a very clear legal and perceptual distinction between NATO and non-NATO uses of Turkish facilities. Given the overwhelming importance of the Alliance link for Turkey, this distinction is unlikely to lose its significance over the coming years. From an American point of view, this argues for giving access requests and proposals for expanded defense cooperation a NATO imprimatur wherever possible. It also reinforces the U.S. interest in NATO's evolution toward a more expansive, global alliance in which Middle Eastern contingencies can be addressed with Ankara in a multilateral manner.

Many contingencies in which access to Turkish bases would be necessary are, in fact, related to the defense of Turkey's own territory. These would be a NATO (Article V) responsibility, although the forces involved would be largely American. The range of such contingencies is potentially quite broad, and embraces ground, air, and missile risks from Syria, Iraq, Iran, and, perhaps under certain conditions, Russia. Under these circumstances, access to Turkish facilities would unquestionably be forthcoming. The more difficult question concerns the nature of day-to-day Western reassurance to Turkey, especially against WMD and missile risks, as this is set to have a more profound influence on the Turkish calculus of risk in future defense cooperation with the United States.[33]

---

[32]Some 55 U.S. aircraft were assigned to Balikesir and Bandirma airbases (together with the refueling base at Corlu) toward the end of Operation Allied Force. Hugh Pope, "Turkey Once Again Becomes Key Strategic Ally of the West," *Wall Street Journal*, May 25, 1999, p. 23.

[33]Ankara will be especially sensitive to developments in this sphere; the August 1999 U.S. decision to withdraw a Patriot battery from the defense of Incirlik sends a very mixed signal at a time when the United States would like to engage Ankara in closer cooperation on theater missile defense. Turkey is also acquiring some new, indigenous capabilities for deterrence and retaliation, including Turkish-manufactured short-range surface-to-surface missiles.

The potential for new progress in the Middle East peace process could improve the outlook for U.S. access to Turkish facilities in non-NATO contingencies by opening the possibility of a coalition approach (as in the Gulf War, but very likely including Israel and Jordan) in which sovereignty issues are diluted. The defense cooperation equation with Turkey is, in this sense, similar to the equation with other European allies. The appearance of "singularization" in cooperation with the United States, especially where the Turkish interest in the use of force is unclear, is no more attractive in Ankara than in Paris or Rome. One motivation for the rapid development of a strategic relationship with Israel has been the Turkish desire for a more diverse set of defense relationships, and opportunities for variable geometry in defense cooperation with the West.

Recent experience, combined with a distinctly nationalist mood in Ankara, argues for caution in U.S. assumptions about the future for Turkey as a power projection partner. But Turkey too has important stakes in cooperation, and these stakes are growing for several reasons. First, the proliferation of conventional and unconventional risks in regions adjacent to Turkey is of a sort that Turkey will find difficult to counter alone, despite its own military modernization program.[34] Even a more militarily capable Europe cannot replace the role of U.S. military power in these (for NATO) far-flung regions. Second, the place of Turkey in nascent European defense arrangements outside NATO is far from clear, even for a Turkey that has become an EU candidate. Ankara has a strong stake in keeping the United States engaged in European and Middle Eastern security, and in the viability of the transatlantic link. The price of keeping the United States engaged in an expeditionary environment will be a clearer understanding with regard to access in regional contingencies.

Third, Turkey's own growing capacity for power projection suggests that future contingencies in the Gulf or elsewhere could see a more active Turkish contribution, countering the perception of Turkey as

---

[34]Planned modernization of conventional forces in Syria and elsewhere in the Middle East, as well as the Caucasus, are part of this equation, as are missile proliferation trends. See "The Caucasus: Racing for Arms," *The Economist,* June 5, 1999, p. 50; and J. David Martin, "Defending Against the Middle Eastern Ballistic Missile Threat," *PolicyWatch* #373 (Washington: WINEP), March 11, 1999.

simply a facilitator with valuable real estate (a harmful perception in Turkish public opinion). The power disparity between the United States and Turkey will inevitably loom large, but need not be as dramatic a factor in public acceptance as in the past. With the second largest military establishment in the Alliance, a vigorous modernization program, and a growing emphasis on mobility, Turkey will be increasingly capable of significant defense contributions in neighboring regions. Finally, and despite clear efforts at diversification, Ankara will have a continuing practical interest in access to U.S. defense systems to support the modernization and restructuring of its forces.[35] Absent significant improvements on human rights and Greek-Turkish relations, the strategic argument about preserving the bilateral relationship will be of leading importance in this regard, especially in Congress. Under these conditions, Ankara will be wary of "letting the U.S. down" in critical contingencies.

This suggests that one key to improving the predictability of bilateral defense cooperation with Turkey is to gain a better understanding of how "critical" contingencies are to be defined, alongside the broader set of regional and functional problems that are amenable to bilateral management and "environment shaping." At the start of the 21st century, there is a trend toward closer bilateral planning in which Turkish interests are not taken for granted. In this setting, the list of contingencies that Washington and Ankara will regard as critical is broadly congruent: threats to existing borders; WMD and ballistic missile risks; and major threats to energy security. These are problems featured in the contemporary Turkish debate on security and strategy, and these are areas where Turkey is most likely to contribute to U.S. freedom of action (the discussion of a new bilateral agenda incorporating these and other issues is taken up in the final chapter of this report).

ELEMENTS OF CONTINUITY AND CHANGE

Despite many complications and constraints, the strategic relationship between Turkey and the United States, and with the West as a

---

[35]U.S. systems Turkey is currently seeking to acquire include 145 attack helicopters, 1,000 main battle tanks, five modern frigates, four AWACS aircraft, and heavy-lift helicopters.

whole, has proven durable in the post–Cold War period. Enduring elements include Turkey's geostrategic position, a tradition of cooperation, and a persistent Western orientation in Turkish foreign policy. Some negative elements (e.g., periodic political instability, a problematic human rights performance, and unresolved tensions with Greece) have proven equally durable as constraints on bilateral and multilateral relations. Also enduring is a relatively underdeveloped sense of U.S. and European affinity with Turkey at the level of public opinion, and among some political elites (changes in this sphere may be one of the positive consequences of the otherwise tragic earthquake of 1999 and its aftermath).

The elements of change, within Turkey and in the strategic environment, are pronounced. Internally, rapid economic growth and attendant social and political strains have left the Atatürkist tradition badly frayed. The authority of the Turkish state is declining (albeit from a very high starting point), accompanied by growing diversity and polarization in Turkish opinion. Public opinion, bolstered by a very active media, also carries greater weight than in the past, with implications for foreign policy and relations with the United States, in particular. Above all, Turkish nationalism has emerged as a potent force on the political scene, just as the quest for eventual Turkish membership in Europe has experienced both setbacks and advances.

At the same time, the international environment has changed in ways that fundamentally change Turkey's strategic importance. Many of the key challenges—and opportunities—are now transregional, emphasizing Turkey's position between increasingly interdependent "regions" (Europe, the Middle East, and Eurasia). NATO and other institutions are in the process of adjusting to this new environment in ways that directly affect Turkish interests and Ankara's utility as a strategic partner. New patterns of cooperation are emerging, including Turkish-Israeli relations, that respond to this new environment and offer Washington new ways of engaging Turkey. Above all, Turkey has shaken off a good deal of its traditional conservatism in foreign and security policy. It is an increasingly self-confident actor, impelled by a much expanded security debate and closer measurement of its own interests. Moreover, extensive defense modernization and restructuring, as well as an expanding web of political and commercial ties, are giving Ankara the ability to act in support of these interests.

POLICY IMPLICATIONS

Anticipating some of the recommendations offered later in this report, what implications can be identified for U.S. policy toward Turkey? Some overall observations can be offered concerning Turkey's internal evolution, its regional role, and its contribution to U.S. freedom of action (the three basic areas of U.S. interest described above).

On the internal scene, the United States should strive to reinforce some positive trends, including a movement away from the dominance of the state in various aspects of Turkish life, the growth of an active debate on domestic and foreign policy, and growing pressure from Turks themselves on human rights and political reform (a force for change that is likely to be far more effective than arm-twisting with Ankara). Although some might see a tension between American strategic interests and democratic imperatives in Turkey, these can more reasonably be seen as mutually reinforcing. A modern, reformist Turkey is also likely to be a more capable and active partner for Washington and the West.[36]

In our engagement with political forces within Turkey, as elsewhere in the Alliance, it will be important to favor elements that reject the renationalization of Turkish external policy. It is worth recognizing, however, that the U.S. ability to influence the domestic evolution of Turkey is extremely, and rightly, limited. Turks will choose for themselves. The United States, with Europe, can help to provide a climate for success. The rise of an influential and policy-aware private sector offers the U.S. opportunities to engage a somewhat broader class of elites, although the Turkish military and the traditional security establishment continues to exert a dominant influence on key foreign and security policy decisionmaking.

Turkey has become a more capable and assertive actor, making the question of Ankara's regional role a more critical one. The thrust of U.S. and Western policy in this regard should be to engage Ankara in a set of multilateral policies (as has been done very successfully in the Balkans), to reduce the attractiveness of options driven by Turk-

---

[36]See Stephen Kinzer, "Between Strategic Interest and Democratic Imperative," *Private View* (Istanbul), Spring 1999, pp. 48–54.

ish nationalism (the United States is not the only NATO ally with uni-
lateralist tendencies). To accomplish this, the balance between
Ankara's Middle Eastern and European roles must be maintained by
vigorously reasserting the post–Cold War Western commitment to
Turkish security, and by assuring—to the extent possible—that
Turkey is not isolated by emerging European defense initiatives.
Continued improvement in Greek-Turkish relations would make an
enormous contribution to the integration of Turkey in European
structures, and would vastly simplify bilateral engagement with
Ankara. At a minimum, Greek-Turkish risk reduction is essential to
avoid the extremely negative consequences for U.S. interests that
would result from open conflict, or even continued brinkmanship
over Cyprus and the Aegean.

Turkey can be a significant contributor to U.S. freedom of action in
critical regions, but a business-as-usual approach to bilateral defense
cooperation faces clear challenges in a climate of rising nationalism
and wariness about unilateral U.S. intervention. Expeditionary requirements are making Turkey more important, but changes in
Turkey and adjacent regions are increasing Ankara's own exposure
and making cooperation less predictable. This dilemma may be
eased through the development of a more diverse relationship in
which defense cooperation is part of a broader web of interests and
initiatives, and through more serious, joint consideration of an
agenda for cooperation in the new strategic environment. In the absence of new rationales and relevant issues for cooperation, an enhanced "strategic relationship"—the stated preference of leaderships
in both countries over the past decade—will remain elusive.

Chapter Five

A STRATEGIC PLAN FOR WESTERN-TURKISH RELATIONS

Zalmay Khalilzad

During the Cold War, Turkey was an important pillar of the Western Alliance. As members of NATO, the United States, Western Europe, and Turkey agreed on the vital objective of opposing Soviet expansion. There was broad agreement among Western Europeans, Turks, and Americans on what they were for and what they were against. Containment of the Soviet Union gave the strategic relationship a clear direction. Since the end of the Cold War, the strategic consensus among the United States, Western Europe, and Turkey has eroded. As described elsewhere in this study, Turkey is very important to Western interests. This chapter identifies four critical common interests for Turkey and the West: ensuring energy security; countering the threat of weapons of mass destruction (WMD) and missiles to Turkey, the adjacent areas, and Western Europe; "congaging"—containing and engaging—Russia; and further integrating Turkey into the West to provide direction for a revitalized strategic alliance between Turkey and its NATO allies.

THE IMPACT OF THE END OF THE COLD WAR

Turkey played a critical role in the containment of Soviet power. Turkey tied down some 24 Soviet divisions and contributed to deterring Moscow from launching a war against NATO.[1] It also provided a platform for the West to monitor Soviet compliance with arms control agreements and related military developments in the Soviet Union. Recognizing that it could not deal with the Soviet threat without support from the West, Ankara worked closely with the United States and key Western European powers.

There was also agreement between the United States and West Germany, in particular, on the central importance of Turkey in Western strategy. A similar recognition of the Turkish role generated support and assistance for Turkey on Capitol Hill. With the end of the Cold War, the geopolitical environment and strategic priorities changed.

In Europe, post–Cold War concern focused on stabilizing the security environment to the east by expanding NATO to East-Central Europe, and on building a new Europe by advancing the political, economic, and security integration of the European Union (EU) nations. Turkey's role in the Gulf War—allowing the use of the Incirlik airbase by U.S. warplanes and supporting the economic embargo against Iraq—demonstrated Turkey's relevance to U.S. strategy in this new era. Many officials in the United States emphasized the increased importance of Turkey. Some have even argued that Turkey's role in the new era could be as important as Germany's during the Cold War.[2]

However, for much of the past decade, there has been a large gap between the rhetoric from Washington on the importance of Turkey and the reality of the bilateral security relationship. In fact, the relative weight of factors complicating security relations between Washington and Ankara has grown, especially on Capitol Hill. As a result, forces opposing strong strategic ties between the United States and Turkey have gained ground. Washington has put obstacles in the way of Turkey's desire to buy American military equipment and, at times, Ankara has felt itself to be under a de facto arms embargo. Military-to-military relations have often been contentious

---

[1]See F. Stephen Larrabee, "U.S. Policy Toward Turkey and the Caspian Basin," in Robert D. Blackwill and Michael Stürmer (eds.), *Allies Divided: Transatlantic Policies Toward the Greater Middle East*, Cambridge: The MIT Press, 1997, pp. 143–173.

[2]Richard Holbrooke, as assistant secretary of state for European and Canadian affairs, was especially active in emphasizing Turkey's role as Europe's new "front line" state.

as demonstrated by persistent U.S. Air Force problems at Incirlik. To express their displeasure with the state of the security relationship, the Turks have at times limited training for U.S. pilots. They have detained equipment and supplies intended for U.S. forces at Incirlik. They have also slowed approval of construction and modernization of facilities and, at times, even restricted flights over northern Iraq. In periods of direct military confrontation with Iraq since the Gulf War, Ankara has generally been unwilling to allow the use of Turkish bases for U.S. air strikes.

Turkey's behavior since the demise of the Soviet threat suggests that it views security cooperation with the United States and key Western European nations as less critical. Turkey no longer faces the colossal threat that the Soviet Union presented. The Turks have become more nationalistic and more sensitive about how their territory and assets are used by the United States.[3]

Turkey's domestic political scene has also complicated "triangular" strategic cooperation with the West. Because of domestic ideological polarization and continued Kurdish unrest, it appeared that Turkey might be headed toward greater instability. These developments led some observers to advocate that the West continue cooperative relations with Turkey, while hedging against some negative outcomes, the potential for which existed as a result of internal trends.[4]

Things have turned out more positively. The Islamist trend has weakened. The PKK has suffered a number of major setbacks. The emergence of a relatively stable coalition in Ankara has created a better climate for political and economic reform. These developments have had a positive effect on Turkey's relations with Europe, as indicated by the 1999 Helsinki decision on Turkey's candidacy for EU membership. Relations with the United States have also improved and become more diverse with new trade and investment opportunities.

---

[3]See Ian Lesser's Chapter Two of this report; see also Lesser, "Turkey's Strategic Options," *International Spectator*, Vol. XXXIV, No. 1 (January-March 1999), pp. 79–88.

[4]For an assessment from the period of Refah's ascendancy, see for example, Simon V. Mayall, *Turkey: Thwarted Ambition*, Washington, DC: National Defense University, January 1997.

However, the triangular relationship between Turkey, Western Europe, and the United States still lacks a clear sense of direction. Uncertainty remains as to what big issues the three, together, can work for, or against, in a new strategic environment.

ELEMENTS OF A NEW STRATEGIC PARTNERSHIP BETWEEN THE UNITED STATES, WESTERN EUROPE, AND TURKEY

Are there objectives that could provide a strong direction for the triangular relationship and shape strategic cooperation for the next 50 years? In particular, can such objectives revitalize relations among the armed forces of the United States, Turkey, and key Western European nations? Our analysis suggests a number of areas that can form the basis of a solid, cooperative relationship for the next decades.

Energy Security

Ensuring the security of energy supplies from the oil-rich Persian Gulf and the Caspian Basin could be adopted as one specific rationale and purpose for the triangular alliance. The Persian Gulf has some 65 percent of the world's known oil resources but is not as big a player when it comes to natural gas. The Caspian Basin has some 3 percent of the world's known oil reserves and some 12 percent of the world's proven natural gas resources.[5]

The Persian Gulf is the critical region in meeting the world's oil needs. In fact, dependence on the Persian Gulf will grow as demands for energy consumption increase because of growth in demand in Asia— particularly China and India. The West will also become more dependent on oil from the region because of increased demand. Energy consumption in the United States and Western Europe is expected to grow by 1.3 percent annually between now and 2015. By the year 2015, 34 percent of North American oil imports will come from the Gulf. In the case of Western Europe, the figure will be 40 percent. Although there are differences in the degree of dependence

---

[5]*International Energy Outlook, 1997,* Washington, DC: Department of Energy, 1998.

on the Gulf, the price of the remaining oil will increase for everyone, should supplies from the Gulf be dramatically reduced.

The direct impact of an interruption in oil supplies on the U.S. and European economies might not be as great as it was during the 1973–74 Arab oil embargo because both are more service oriented than they were in the 1970s. The U.S. and several European nations now have strategic petroleum reserves that could cushion the impact of any embargo or interruptions. Both have also diversified their energy dependence. By comparison, the impact on the weak democracies and emerging economies could be far more severe. Nevertheless, a prolonged interruption in the supply of energy from the Gulf would result in dramatic increases in oil prices and have a negative impact on the U.S., European, and Asian economies. The Persian Gulf will be the key to energy security in the coming decades because its oil is cheap to extract, the reserves are large, and there is significant existing and potential production capacity.

The world potentially faces two types of challenges to oil security in the Gulf: interruption of oil supplies because of internal or regional conflicts or the domination of the region by a hostile power. Interruption could take place in several scenarios—for example, an Iraqi or Iranian attack against one or more Gulf Cooperation Council (GCC) states; attacks against major oil facilities using WMD; a conflict inside Saudi Arabia that includes the oil-producing region; or terrorist attacks against major oil-producing facilities.

Oil supplies from the Gulf might also be interrupted if the region came to be dominated by a hostile power. A hostile hegemon might use the income from oil to build its military capability and expand its political influence to pose a broader challenge. It might use oil as a vehicle for blackmail, to seek concessions on political issues or the transfer of technology, or to split allies. In the past, both Iran and Iraq have sought regional hegemony. Both continue to have such ambitions. Because of the U.S. military presence in the region and the relative capabilities of both countries, prospects for regional hegemony by Iran or Iraq are remote. Unless the U.S. abandons the region, the likely threats are terrorism and limited military attacks against the GCC states, including their oil facilities. For planning purposes, a U.S., European, and Turkish agreement to provide security for energy supplies from the Gulf would have to include not only measures to deal with these smaller threats, but also to deter or defeat an invasion of the GCC states by Iraq and Iran.

As of now, the United States, as the Persian Gulf's ultimate security guarantor, has assumed the responsibility for defending access to the region's oil supplies. The United States has deployed forces in the GCC states and the surrounding areas for this purpose. However, the disproportionate U.S. burden in defending the region might not be sustainable if the costs of playing such a role increase, and because of other U.S. commitments around the world. Burden sharing has been a contentious issue in the Alliance. It may become even more so. Since Turkey and Western European nations are more dependent on Persian Gulf oil than the United States, the United States might expect them to contribute their fair share to ensure the security of energy supplies.

While the Gulf is critical to future energy security, the Caspian Basin can also play a significant role and should not be ignored. Compared to the Gulf, the region has much less oil, production costs are much higher, and the cost of exports will be significantly higher. Nevertheless, it can assist in diversifying supplies. For Turkey's own energy security, the region could become vitally important. If the current plans for bringing oil and gas from the region to Turkey materialize, Ankara will become critically dependent on the Caspian Basin.

A key part of the Turkish plan is to build the Baku-Ceyhan pipeline, which would bring Caspian oil and gas across Turkey. The United States and Turkey have been very vocal supporters of the project. However, the Turks, Western Europeans, and Americans have not been serious about building the pipeline. The initiative has been left largely to the private sector, and the energy companies involved are understandably reluctant to move ahead with such a costly project if the economics of the scheme are uncertain. If current trends hold, it is unlikely to be built.

The reason for supporting the project has been geopolitical: to bolster Turkey's regional role; to orient the exporting countries toward the West and to consolidate their independence from Russia; to discourage increased reliance on Iran and the Straits of Hormuz (likely if future supplies are shipped via the "cheaper" route from the Caspian region to Iran's Gulf coast); and to reduce the environmental risks of increased tanker traffic through the Black Sea and the Bosphorus. Given these considerations, and compared with the alternatives, the United States, Western Europe, and Turkey should be prepared to subsidize the construction of the Baku-Ceyhan pipeline across Turkey, offsetting the attractiveness of less expensive but strategically unwise alternatives. The investment can be justified in geopolitical terms, and can be one of the first steps in focusing the Turkish-European-American alliance on a new agenda on which energy security figures prominently.

The Turks already consider the Caspian Basin as very important because of ethnic ties and geographic proximity. Energy dependence will make the region even more important. The Caspian Basin is also potentially very unstable because of internal factors in each of the key energy-producing countries, threats of regional conflicts, and possible intervention from outside the region.

In order to get Turkish cooperation to provide security for energy supplies from the Persian Gulf, and because of the importance of the Caspian Basin, the West should be more attentive to Turkish stakes in the security of the region and work with Ankara to promote its political and economic development. Should the alliance between Turkey, the United States, and Western European nations be revitalized along the lines proposed here, Turkey will become even more central in strategic terms. It will be unrealistic to regard Turkey as critically important in the energy security equation, and yet ignore the Caspian Basin which Turkey regards as critical to its own interests.

Turkey is ideally located to play a vital role to ensure security both in the Persian Gulf and in the Caspian Basin. Turkish military facilities provide an excellent location for projecting power to both regions. For example, the bulk of Persian Gulf and Caspian energy resources are within 1,000 miles of Incirlik.

An agreement between Turks, Europeans, and Americans on energy security will provide one clear, strategic direction for relations, and should focus on planning and developing scenarios to deal with these issues jointly. It will also provide a basis to determine the kind of forces that each will need for missions related to ensuring energy security, and the kind of presence and facilities the United States and

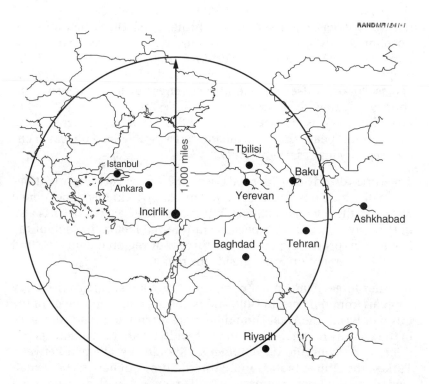

RANDMR1241-1

Figure 1—Turkey-Persian Gulf and Caspian Basin

the Europeans would need in Turkey. Such a development can also offer new flexibility in planning the U.S. military presence in adjacent regions. For example, access to Turkish bases can reduce the amount of military presence required in some of the GCC states.

Countering the Threat of Weapons of Mass Destruction and Missiles

Western Europe, the United States, and Turkey have a strong shared interest in countering the spread of WMD and ballistic missiles.

The regions adjacent to Turkey pose one of the greatest challenges to the global nonproliferation regime. Missiles of ever increasing ranges and WMD are spreading in the region. The Missile Technology Control Regime (MTCR) has not prevented their spread. Already, Iraq, Iran, Syria, Saudi Arabia, and reportedly Armenia, have ballistic missiles that can reach Turkish targets.[6] Several countries, such as Iran, have plans for longer-range missiles and nuclear weapons.

Since Desert Storm, the attractiveness of acquiring ballistic missiles and WMD, especially nuclear and radiological weapons, has increased. Iraqi missiles provided Saddam Hussein with significant leverage over the United States and Israel. During Desert Storm, the United States faced major difficulties in dealing with Iraqi mobile missiles. Some countries appear to believe that such capabilities would lessen the likelihood that the United States would use force against them, or use force in a way that could impose a decisive defeat, even if they were to challenge U.S. interests. Some believe that this type of capability offers weaker hostile states the ability to compete with the United States asymmetrically—investing in cheap technologies that negate or lessen U.S. advantages.[7]

Regional incentives—the competition between Iran and Iraq, Pakistan and Iran, Saudi Arabia and Iran, Israel and several Middle East states, and Syria and Turkey—are probably more important.[8] Some believe that missiles and WMD can affect the outcome of war by undermining the rival's other advantages. Another reason for increased interest in WMD and missiles is that the cost of modernizing conventional forces has increased significantly. Many potentially hostile states are in such economic condition that they cannot afford large-scale conventional modernization.

In the future, the relative importance of this issue will grow. First, continued Turkish vulnerability to missiles deployed by hostile governments will increase Ankara's incentive to either acquire defenses against such missiles, in cooperation with its Western allies, or to acquire its own missiles and deterrent capabilities. Turkey has ex-

---

[6]Armenia is reported to possess a number of SCUD missiles. See *The Military Balance 1999–2000*, London: International Institute for Strategic Studies, 1999. Russia, Israel, and Egypt also possess capable missile systems in the Turkish neighborhood.

[7]*New World Coming: American Security in the 21st Century*, Arlington, VA: U.S. Commission on National Security/21st Century, 1999, p. 49.

[8]See Ian O. Lesser and Ashley J. Tellis, *Strategic Exposure: Proliferation Around the Mediterranean*, Santa Monica, CA: RAND, MR-742-A, 1996.

pressed interest in missile defenses, and is having more detailed discussions with key allies, including the United States and Israel, on missile defense technologies and architecture. Turkey is also embarking on the design and production of its own short-range missiles, and could move to develop longer-range systems. Turkey's incentives to develop its own retaliatory capabilities, as opposed to defensive efforts, will depend critically on the health of the strategic relationship with the United States and NATO. Ankara seeks reassurance that the NATO security guarantee, including its nuclear dimension, remains valid in the face of a more diverse set of post–Cold War risks to Turkish territory.

Second, although Turkey is now the NATO ally most exposed to missile and WMD risks, it is only a question of time before West European cities can be attacked with missiles armed with WMD from hostile regional states on Europe's southern periphery, and sooner or later, Europeans will have to worry about homeland vulnerability. This change is likely to take place in the next 10 years.[9] Europe's vulnerability to WMD and missile attacks from the Middle East could have grave consequences. The ability of Europeans, Americans, and Turks to cooperate to defeat threats to common interests (e.g., energy security) might well be impaired if hostile regimes hold Istanbul, Rome, Paris, Berlin, and London hostage to retaliatory attacks.[10] Aggressors might well believe that Turks, or other Western allies, will not trade their cities for Kuwait or Riyadh. The possibility of this type of retaliation will complicate any unilateral military action by the United States even if North American cities are not vulnerable. At a minimum, this exposure to the retaliatory consequences of Western intervention will sharpen debates about access and defense cooperation with NATO allies, especially Turkey. Finally, in the longer term, even U.S. cities will become vulnerable to missiles launched from areas near Turkey.

Within the Alliance, Turkey and the United States take the threat of the spread of missiles and WMD to the areas adjacent to Turkey most seriously. They are alarmed. But European perceptions differ. In

---

[9]Ibid.

[10]Zalmay Khalilzad, "Challenges in the Greater Middle East," in Gompert and Larrabee (eds.), *Europe and America*, pp. 205–206.

general, Europeans, including some already within range of current systems, have yet to be convinced of the seriousness of the problem. This may change as the missile capability of countries such as Iran increases and as Europe becomes more vulnerable to missile attacks.

There are already some signs that the danger is being acknowledged. The new NATO strategic concept stresses the missile threat to NATO countries. Some joint committees have been established, including the Defense Group on Proliferation, the Senior Group on Proliferation, and the Weapons of Mass Destruction Center. A serious effort will have to focus on mission development plans, capabilities, and concept of operations. The United States is making a significant effort. Europe, too, is moving toward a multilayered missile defense system, but at NATO speed, in part, because many Europeans are still uncomfortable with military approaches to proliferation risks. Security elites in Ankara do not share this discomfort.

Turkey can play a critical role, not only for its own defense, but as part of a coordinated group with Europe, the United States, and friendly regional states such as Israel, Jordan, Egypt, and Saudi Arabia. For its own defense and the defense of U.S. forces and friends in the area, antitactical missile systems could be based in Turkey or its territorial waters. The best defense would be a Boost Phase Intercept system which can also help with deterrence, since part of the attacking missile will fall in the country launching it. As part of the missile defense architecture for Europe, early warning systems could be placed in Turkey and in some Middle Eastern countries. Some of the systems for intercepting longer-range missiles launched against Western Europe could also be stationed in Turkey—an arrangement that would usefully reinforce Turkish defense ties with both NATO and emerging EU security institutions.

"Congage" Russia

Russia's future remains uncertain and, at present, it is neither an ally nor an enemy of the United States, Europe, and Turkey. The political, economic, and military forces that will shape Russia's future can produce a variety of outcomes—some positive and some very negative. As a democratic state, Russia should be expected to follow a generally cooperative strategy similar to that followed by other democratic powers, primarily focused on increasing the welfare of its citizens and cooperating with the current international system. It could become increasingly democratic and integrated as a positive contributor to regional peace and stability. However, the process of democratization could be protracted and could be accompanied by a more aggressive Russian nationalism. This is already visible in the aftermath of the Kosovo crisis and the Russian assault on Chechnya.

Alternatively, Russia could face a major domestic crisis, and collapse into chaos and disintegration. As the conflict in Chechnya demonstrates, some regions in the country are resentful of the center. The country faces many political, economic, and social problems that, without a democratically oriented leadership, could strengthen centrifugal forces and destabilize the state.

A third outcome is the possibility of a strong authoritarian leadership. Such a leadership might seek to restore its lost empire, at least in some form, and pursue policies hostile to the United States, Turkey, and Europe. Many in Russia are dissatisfied with the current international system, in which the United States, as the only "superpower," often seeks to act in a "hegemonic" manner. Replacing the current international system with a multipolar one, in which Russia will be one of several relatively equal powers, is a declared objective of Russian policy.

Should Russia become aggressive and expansionist, the Caspian Basin is likely to become a target of such activism. In the aftermath of the recent Russian war in Chechnya, there is a significant rise in the perception of a Russian threat in surrounding regions, particularly Azerbaijan, Georgia, and Central Asia. A number of these countries face domestic instability and succession problems, and are vulnerable to Russian manipulations. Russian expansion in the Caspian Basin and Central Asia will pose significant problems for Turkish and Western interests.

As long as Russia's future is uncertain, neither pure engagement nor containment is an adequate Western strategy toward Moscow. Engagement rests on the hope that economic, political, and military connections will transform Russia into a cooperative democracy or, at a minimum, produce convergence on some key interests. This is a supposition. Should Russia become a hostile authoritarian state, a policy of engagement will merely have made Russia into a potentially more threatening adversary.

But shifting to containment is troublesome. Such a strategy presupposes that Russia would ultimately become hostile, ignoring the possibility that Western-Russian relations could evolve in a more cooperative direction. Containment could become a self-fulfilling prophecy, setting the stage for a confrontation where none existed.

Neither engagement nor containment balances the two key Western objectives, which should be to encourage Russia to become more democratic and cooperative while at the same time protecting Western interests by hedging against the possibility that Russia might become more hostile. Such a strategy could be called "congagement."[11] It would continue to assist and encourage political and economic reform and seek to integrate Russia into the current international system, while both preparing for a possible Russian challenge to this system, and seeking to convince the Russian leadership that any such challenge would be difficult to mount and risky to pursue.

Under congagement, we would enhance military, economic, and political relations with Russia. However, we would criticize disturbing aspects of Russian domestic and foreign behavior more vigorously. When Moscow threatens Western interests, we must be prepared to respond. NATO expansion to East-Central Europe is a good hedge against Russia becoming hostile and imposing hegemony in that region and the nearby areas. In addition, as a hedge against a potentially hostile Russia, the United States, Europe, and Turkey should move on two fronts:

First, we should avoid doing anything that directly helps the growth of Russian military power. Existing U.S. and allied export controls that now restrict access to Western technology need to be strengthened. This will be an important point for discussion with Ankara as

---

[11] The term "congagement" is offered as a theme for U.S. strategy toward China in Zalmay Khalilzad et al., *The United States and a Rising China: Strategic and Military Implications,* Santa Monica, CA: RAND, MR-1082, 1999. The term is equally relevant to the question of policy toward Russia.

Turkey seeks to diversify its own sources of military technology and develops more extensive contacts with Russia.[12]

Second, deterring Russian expansionism in the Caspian Basin and Central Asia (and perhaps a more aggressive stance in the Balkans and the eastern Mediterranean), and planning a response to such expansion, should become a core focus of policy and defense planning between Europe, the United States, and Turkey. Dealing with potential Russian threats to this region requires many steps, including measures to enhance ties with states in the Caspian Basin and Central Asia. New formal alliance relationships, such as expansion of NATO to the region, are neither necessary nor practical at this time. However, in the aftermath of the war in Chechnya, and especially in light of the brutal way in which the operation was conducted, it would be prudent to expand security cooperation, including enhanced military-to-military relations with key states such as Azerbaijan, Georgia, and Uzbekistan. In addition, it would be important to promote regional cooperation including the settlement of local disputes among the states of the area along the lines of the Caucasus "pact" proposed by Ankara.

These steps are important in themselves for deterrence and regional stability, but they can also assist to toughen policy toward Russia should this become necessary. It is not in the interest of the United States, Turkey, and Western Europe for Russia to dominate this region. A congagement strategy would sharpen the choice faced by Russian leaders. If Russia cooperates with the current international system, seeks cooperation rather than hegemony in regions such as the Caspian Basin, and becomes increasingly democratic, this policy could evolve into mutual accommodation and partnership. If Russia becomes a hostile power bent on regional domination, this policy can shift toward containment.

Congagement of Russia is an area where Turkey has much to contribute and also has a strong stake in Western reassurance and deter-

---

[12]Examples include Turkish consideration of attack helicopter purchases from a Russian-Israeli consortium, and possible joint production of S-300 surface-to-air missiles. In the past, Ankara has purchased support helicopters and armored personnel carriers from Russia. See Lale Sariibrahimoglu, "Russia Offers Turkey S-300 Production Deal," *Jane's Defence Weekly*, March 8, 2000.

rence. As with proliferation risks, Ankara worries more than its NATO allies about the possibility of a renewed competition with Russia. History plays a role here, together with the sense that a new cold war with Moscow would likely take the form of friction on Russia's southern periphery rather than a more direct confrontation in Europe. Ankara is concerned that it could be left to face such "flank risks" alone. At the same time, Turkey has an important stake in stability and reform in Russia, not least because Russia has emerged as a leading economic partner, especially important to meet Turkey's ever growing energy needs. All of this suggests that strategy toward a changing Russia will be one of the key points for coordination between Ankara and its Western security partners.

Deepening Turkish Integration in the West

Integrating Turkey into the EU should be an important objective of the future strategic cooperation between the United States, Europe, and Turkey. Most Turks are interested in reinforcing ties to the West, and deepening the relationship with the EU. The United States favors Turkey's eventual full membership in the EU for the following reasons:

- Integrating a state that favors strong transatlantic ties into the EU can have a positive effect on how EU-U.S. relations evolve over the long term;

- Preparing for and joining the EU will have a positive effect on Turkey's own evolution as a secular, Western-oriented democracy;

- This, in turn, will improve prospects for strategic cooperation of the kind discussed above between Turkey, the United States, and Europe.

Whereas the United States tends to take a strategic view of the rationale for Turkish membership, EU members pay relatively greater attention to how Turkey fits in Europe's economic, political, and even cultural order. Turkey's size exacerbates these issues and suggests that the road to Turkish membership will not be straight or easy. It could end in a closer Turkish-EU relationship that stops short of full membership. Or the EU itself may evolve into a multispeed, multilevel institution with more options for Turkey. Turks, too, will have their reservations about the sovereignty compromises inherent in EU membership. The key point from the "triangular" point of view is to ensure that the path toward Europe remains open and gives Turkey a legitimate Euro-Atlantic role. Ankara must not be shut out. As Europe and the United States focus more heavily on challenges in Turkey's neighborhood, the West, as a whole, has a stronger stake in ensuring that Turkey's integration is strengthened and made irreversible.

Because Turkish integration is important, the United States should continue to encourage its Europeans allies to put real substance behind the Helsinki summit decision on Turkey's candidacy for EU membership. If the Helsinki decision turns out to be a hollow commitment, it could harm prospects for Turkish cooperation with the West, and would strengthen those Turks who favor other options. It is up to the Europeans how they proceed on the EU membership, and it is up to Turks to take the steps necessary for accession. The United States can put the case for Turkish membership on strategic grounds, but it has no standing to decide the outcome. Washington would have to move delicately so as not to harm Turkey's prospects.

While Turkish membership in the EU is the ultimate answer to the question of integrating Turkey into the West, there are interim issues that must be addressed in the near future. Like the United States, Turkey is concerned about the evolution of the European Security and Defense Identity (ESDI) and emerging European power projection arrangements. The United States should work with Europe to make sure that Turkey is not excluded. Defense issues may actually evolve more easily between Turkey and the EU, compared with some of the other issues that must be resolved on the way to deeper Turkish integration in Europe. But, in the immediate future, assisting with the resolution of the defense issues and preventing discrimination against Turkey must become a principal U.S. concern. Turks too will view this aspect of the relationship with Europe as a key test of the EU's willingness to integrate Turkey.

Closer Turkish integration in Europe will encourage a constructive diversification of Turkish-Western relations outside the security realm. This diversification should also apply to the bilateral relationship with the United States. Although Europe will undoubtedly be the most important economic partner for Ankara over the next decades, there will also be opportunities to strengthen trade and investment with U.S. partners. The energy sector is already emerging as a leader in this respect with, for example, significant new business in the power-generation field. A more prosperous Turkey, with a streamlined set of regulations governing foreign investment and arbitration, more closely harmonized with European practices, will create a more attractive environment for American business activity in the country. In short, a more European Turkey can facilitate Turkey's development as a "big emerging market" as seen from Washington.

CONCLUSION

Turkey, the United States, and Europe have important common interests: energy security, counterproliferation, "congaging" Russia and integrating Turkey into the West. These common interests call for a more ambitious triangular partnership. As a first step, the three must reexamine the status of the Baku-Ceyhan pipeline and develop a strategy for generating the financial resources necessary for making it happen. Future security relations, objectives, strategies, and institutions should be organized around these interests and in a new revitalized alliance. This should affect several institutions: NATO, the EU, and bilateral American-Turkish arrangements.

The new NATO strategic concept is a step in the right direction, and provides a better basis for triangular security cooperation. But it does not go far enough. For example, energy security and scenarios that might undermine it must be a direct focus for the Alliance, and provide the guidance needed by force planners.

For Turkey, too, a partnership focused on these four major interests will have important implications. The Turks talk about these issues in a serious manner. But will they accept the responsibilities associated with it—such as the reconfiguration of allied military presence on their territory? It serves their interests to do so. They cannot protect these interests alone. And unless they play a role in protecting important common interests, the security dimension of the relationship will continue to erode.

The U.S. role—as the leader and the catalyst for refocusing the relationship between the United States, Europe, and Turkey on these core interests—is critical. Without such a role by the United States, the necessary adaptation in American-Turkish-European relations will not take place, and the West as a whole will be less well equipped to address some of the most important new challenges on the international scene.